Knitting
Around
the World

from *Threads*

Knitting Around the World

from *Threads*

The Taunton Press

Cover photo courtesy of Elizabeth Zimmermann.
The garments shown are historical pieces for which
no patterns are available. See pp. 21-25 for information
on Bohus knitting.

Taunton
BOOKS & VIDEOS

for fellow enthusiasts

First printing: June 1993
Second printing: June 1994
Printed in the United States of America

A THREADS Book

THREADS® is a trademark of The Taunton Press, Inc.,
registered in the U.S. Patent and Trademark Office.

The Taunton Press
63 South Main Street
Box 5506
Newtown, CT 06470-5506

Library of Congress Cataloging-in-Publication Data

Knitting around the world from Threads.
    p. cm.
   "A Threads book" — CIP t.p. verso.
   Includes index.
   ISBN 1-56158-026-0
   1. Knitting. 2. Knitting — Patterns.
TT820.K6965 1993   93-22204
746.43'2 — dc20   CIP

Contents

Introduction

or a craft with just two basic stitches – knit and purl – knitting demonstrates a mind-boggling diversity and intricacy, as well as a rich international tradition. Here are the examples to prove it, gathered from the issues of *Threads* magazine, including: cabled Aran sweaters from off the coast of Ireland; Shetland lace shawls of such finely spun wool that the gossamer wraps slip through a wedding ring; Spanish lace doilies and how to starch them; contemporary Japanese knitting that intertwines custom dyeing with meticulous technique and a relatively new system of charting stitches; Fair Isle two-color knitting; and Swedish knitting from both ends of a ball of yarn. The variations go on and on.

And last, but only the beginning of more discoveries, knitters from Scotland, Germany, France, Norway and Greece share how they hold their needles.

Amy T. Yanagi, editor

Aran Knitting

Intricately textured sweaters built around the simple cable

by Alice Starmore

Illustrations by Mark Kara

This child's sweater is an example of the traditional Aran fishing sweater. There is a cabled center panel flanked by narrower side panels on the front (facing page), back (above), and sleeves.

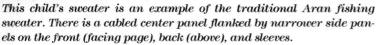

n Aran sweater is a master-piece of beauty combined with practicality. By crossing and twisting their stitches in the style of Celtic patterns, Aran knitters maximize the insulating properties of the wool without sacrificing its elasticity, and create aesthetically pleasing garments to boot.

Aran knitting relies substantially on cable patterns to create its complex relief surfaces. Cable stitches are simple to execute, but they can be combined in ingenious ways to produce the intricate patterns we recognize as Aran knitting. Information on how to work a cable and several examples of simple and complex cable patterns are provided on pages 10-13.

History

There is no question that the unique and intricate knitting style known as Aran knitting began on the Aran Islands. Aside from this fact, however, there are no definite clues to the date or circumstances of its origin. The Aran Islands consist of three

small islands: Inishmore, Inishmaan and Inisheer, situated in the mouth of Galway Bay on the west coast of the Republic of Ireland. The environment is harsh and inhospitable, consisting mainly of barren rock interspersed with small pieces of fertile land that are continuously swept by the salt-laden Atlantic winds. Survival here was possible only by constant effort and skill-ful utilization of the sparse resources. The sea was the mainstay, providing a rich abundance of fish. The men were brave and skilled fishermen, putting out to sea in their curraghs—elementary canvas-covered craft capable of surviving in heavy waters. Seaweed was hauled from the shore to enrich the soil for growing potatoes, rye, and oats and for feeding cattle and sheep. Stone provided material for houses and walls.

The islanders not only provided all their own food and shelter, but they also manufactured their clothing. Sheep wool was used to weave homespun tweed, known as *bainin* (pronounced *bawneen*). The men wove colorful belts (*criosannas*), which they

wore around their waists. Rawhide was used to make shoes (*pampooties*), which had to be dampened periodically so they would stay supple.

The islanders had no need or time for the written word, but their lifestyle, economy, and mode of dress have been well described by visitors. It is interesting that those who have given detailed accounts, like Samuel Lewis in his *Topographical Dictionary* (1837) and J. M. Synge in his book *The Aran Islands* (1907), did not mention any unusual knitting. Indeed, Aran knitting was first discovered by Heinze Kiewe, who purchased an Aran sweater in a Dublin shop in 1936. He showed this unusual sweater to Mary Thomas, then fashion editor of the *Morning Post,* and she published an Aran pattern in *Mary Thomas's Book of Knitting Patterns* in 1943. Both Kiewe and Thomas did a great deal to publicize and popularize the art. Kiewe in particular devoted a great deal of time to collecting and notating the patterns, which had never be-

(continued on page 13)

Six-stitch Rope Cables. Left to right: back crossed on the 8th and 12th rows alternately, back crossed on every 8th row, front crossed on every 6th row.

Cables combining back and front cross. Left to right: OXO Cable, Honeycomb Cable, Wave Cable, Reverse Double Cable, Double Cable.

Cable patterns

All cable patterns are formed by one simple technique—the crossing of one stitch or a group of stitches over another stitch or group of stitches. A cable needle is usually used to hold the first half of the stitches while the second half is knit. The stitches from the cable needle are then knit. The drawings below of six-stitch Rope Cables show the techniques.

Rope Cables are the most basic form of cable knitting and are often used to frame larger patterns on Aran sweaters. The rope is worked on an even number of stitches in stockinette stitch on a textured, usually purl, background. Continuous back crossing forms a rope twisting to the right, while continuous front crossing forms a rope twisting to the left.

Rope Cables can vary in width—2 sts, 4 sts, 6 sts, etc.—up to 12 sts—about the maximum with an Aran yarn and a firm gauge without the crossed stitches looking strained. The number of rows worked between cable cross rows can also vary. To produce a classic rope, work the same number of rows as there are stitches: Cross a 4-st cable every 4th row; a 6-st cable, every 6th row, etc. Make a slightly looser rope by working two more rows than there are stitches—cross a 4-st cable every 6th row or an 8-st cable every 10th row. The photo at top left shows a variety of six-stitch Rope Cables.

Next in the development of cable patterns are the cables that employ both front and back crosses. The simplest is the *Double Cable,* which is, in effect, a back-cross cable and a front-cross cable placed side by side with no background stitches between. To knit a Double Cable with 2 purl sts at each side, cast on 12 sts. Work as follows:
Rows 1, 3, 5, 7 (wrong side): K2, p8, k2.
Row 2: P2, sl2 to cn and hold at back, k2, then k2 from cn; sl2 to cn and hold at front, k2, then k2 from cn; p2.

Rows 4, 6, 8: P2, k8, p2.
Rep rows 1 to 8.

You can work a *Reverse Double Cable* by reading on Row 2 "hold at front" instead of "hold at back," and vice versa. The widths of the Double Cable or Reverse Double Cable can be varied, but the total number must be divisible by 4 so that each half of the cable has an equal number of stitches. The lengths between cable cross rows can also vary.

The *Wave Cable* is a simple example of the use of front cross and back cross on alternate cable cross rows. To knit a Wave Cable with 2 purl sts at each side, cast on 10 sts and work as follows:
Row 1 (wrong side) and all wrong-side rows: K2, p6, k2.
Row 2: P2, sl3 to cn and hold at back, k3, then k3 from cn; p2.
Rows 4, 6: P2, k6, p2.
Row 8: P2, sl3 sts to cn and hold at front, k3, then k3 from cn; p2.
Rows 10, 12: P2, k6, p2.
Rep rows 1 to 12.

When you work the Wave Cable at each side of a common center pattern, start one cable at row 1 and the other at row 7 so the waves mirror one another. Widths and lengths can be varied.

The *Honeycomb Cable* is composed of two 4-st Wave Cables placed side by side mirroring each other. To knit a Honeycomb Cable with 2 purl sts at each side, cast on 12 sts. Work as follows:
Row 1 and all wrong-side rows: K2, p8, k2.
Row 2: P2, sl2 to cn and hold at back, k2, then k2 from cn (BC); sl2 to cn and hold at front, k2, then k2 from cn (FC); p2.
Row 4: P2, k8, p2.
Row 6: P2, FC, BC, p2.
Row 8: P2, k8, p2.
Rep rows 1 to 8.

The Honeycomb Cable is the basis for the *Honeycomb Stitch,* which is a number of Honeycomb Cables repeated over multiples of 8 sts. This is a favorite pattern for the center panels. To knit

Honeycomb Stitch.

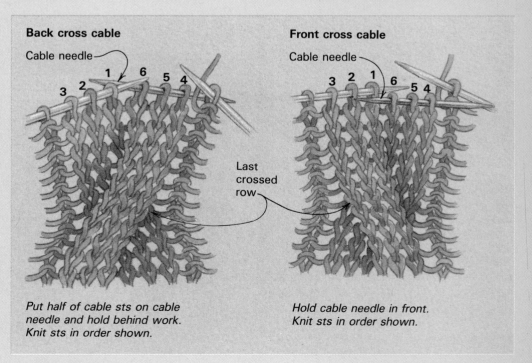

Back cross cable

Cable needle

3 2 1 6 5 4

Put half of cable sts on cable needle and hold behind work. Knit sts in order shown.

Front cross cable

Cable needle

3 2 1 6 5 4

Last crossed row

Hold cable needle in front. Knit sts in order shown.

the pattern, cast on a multiple of 8 sts and work as follows:

Row 1 and all wrong-side rows: Purl.
Row 2: BC, FC; rep across.
Row 4: Knit.
Row 6: FC, BC; rep across.
Row 8: Knit.
Rep rows 1 to 8.
You can elongate both the Honeycomb Cable and the Honeycomb Stitch by working 2 more rows between each cable cross row.

OXO Cable is a variation of the Honeycomb Cable and demonstrates how a change in cable cross-row order can produce a different result. Read BC and FC as explained for the Honeycomb Cable. To knit an OXO Cable with 2 purl sts at each side, cast on 12 sts.
Rows 1, 3 (wrong side): K2, p8, k2.
Row 2: P2, k8, p2.
Row 4: P2, BC, FC, p2.
Rows 5, 6, 7: Rep rows 1, 2, 3.
Row 8: P2, FC, BC, p2.
Rows 9 to 12: Rep rows 5 to 8.
Rows 13 to 16: Rep rows 1 to 4.
Rep rows 1 to 16.

Front and back crosses are used effectively to open out patterns, creating diamond and curved shapes, which can be filled with a variety of textured patterns. The **Moss Stitch Diamond** is the classic Aran example where, after the base of the diamond has been established (row 2), front and back crosses move the cable outward by 1 st on each right-side row. The diamond is then closed when the cable is moved inward by 1 st on each right-side row. To knit a Moss Stitch Diamond, cast on 15 sts. Work as follows:
Row 1 (wrong side): K5, p2, k1, p2, k5.
Row 2: P5; sl3 to cn and hold at front, k2, then slip the purl st from cn to left needle (ln) and purl it, k2 from cn; p5.
Row 3: Same as row 1.
Row 4: P4; sl1 to cn and hold at back, k2, purl the st from cn (BC); k1; sl2 to cn and hold at front, p1, then k2 from cn (FC); p4.
Row 5 and all following wrong-side rows: Knit all knit sts; purl all purl sts.
Row 6: P3, BC, k1, p1, k1, FC, p3.
Row 8: P2, BC, (k1, p1) 2x, k1, FC, p2.
Row 10: P1, BC, (k1, p1) 3x, k1, FC, p1.
Row 12: BC, (k1, p1) 4x, k1, FC.
Row 14: FC, (p1, k1) 4x, p1, BC.
Row 16: P1, FC, (p1, k1) 3x, p1, BC, p1.
Row 18: P2, FC, (p1, k1) 2x, p1, BC, p2.
Row 20: P3, FC, p1, k1, p1, BC, p3.
Row 22: P4, FC, p1, BC, p4.
Rep rows 1 to 22.

You can achieve a curved shape by working 3 or 5 rows straight before closing the cable inward. To work an open cable like the cables on each side of the Moss Stitch Diamond, open the cable until there are 5 purl center sts, and then work 3 rows straight before closing the cable.

With open cables there is infinite scope for variation, and some motifs are rather simple. For example, you can work the diamond with cable borders of 1 st instead of 2 sts, or you can work row 2 twice, for a double twist between each diamond.

More complex variations include the **Moss Stitch Diamond Trellis,** another familiar Aran pattern often used as a

Moss Stitch Diamond with open cables at each side.

Moss Stitch Diamond Trellis.

Fivefold Aran Braid.

Ribbed Cable.

Openwork Fan.

center panel. You work it by placing two Moss Stitch Diamonds side by side. In other words, work the classic diamond twice over 30 sts. The inside borders of each diamond will meet when they have been fully opened out. Then cross the border stitches over one another (with either a back or a front cross) on the following right-side row. Close both diamonds as usual. This forms a center purl-stitch diamond which, unlike the Moss Stitch Diamonds, will have an even number of stitches. If you knit the first 4 inside sts, you can work a 4-st cable up the center of the diamond.

These are just a few examples of the variations possible with open cables. Once you have understood and practiced the technique, trying out your own can be creative and great fun.

To make the **Fivefold Aran Braid,** you use the back cross as in row 2 of the diamond, and also its counterpart front cross. The pattern is dense and similar to basic Celtic interlacing. The braid is worked over a panel of 18 sts as follows:
Row 1 (wrong side): K2, (p2, k1) 4x, p2, k2.
Row 2: 2, (k2, p1) 4x, k2, p2.
Row 3 and all following wrong-side rows: Same as row 1.

Row 4: P2, k2, (p1, sl3 to cn and hold at front, k2, then slip the purl st back to ln and purl it, k2 from cn) 2x, p2.
Row 6: Same as row 2.
Row 8: P2, (sl3 to cn and hold at back, k2, then slip the purl st back to ln and purl it, k2 from cn, p1) 2x, k2, p2.
Rep rows 1 to 8.

Other simple techniques create different effects. Knitting into the back of a knit stitch (kb) on the right side and purling into the back of the same stitch (pb) on the wrong side results in a twisted stitch with a corded look. It is effective in cable borders, such as the Moss Stitch Diamond, or in rib patterns, of which the **Ribbed Cable** is a classic example. The Ribbed Cable is worked over 11 sts, as follows:
Row 1 (wrong side): K2, (p1b, k1) 3x, p1b, k2.
Row 2: P2, sl3 to cn and hold at front, (k1b, p1) 2x over next 4 sts, then k1b, p1, k1b from cn, p2.
Rows 3, 5, 7, 9: Same as row 1.
Rows 4, 6, 8, 10: P2, (k1b, p1) 3x, k1b, p2.
Rep rows 1 to 10.

For a back cross Ribbed Cable, work Row 2 as follows: P2, sl4 to cn and hold at back, k1b, p1, k1b over next 3 sts, then (p1, k1b) 2x from cn, p2.

Another simple technique combines cable with slip stitch. The most popular example of this technique is the **Wishbone Cable,** which is often used to frame larger panels. To knit the Wishbone Cable with 2 purl sts at each side, cast on 10 sts and work as follows:
Row 1 (wrong side): K2, p6, k2.
Row 2: P2, k2, sl2 with yarn in back, k2, p2.
Row 3: K2, p2, sl2 with yarn in front, p2, k2.
Row 4: P2, sl2 to cn and hold at back, k1, then k2 from cn; sl1 to cn and hold at front, k2, then k1 from cn; p2.
Rep rows 1 to 4.

Although openwork patterns aren't generally associated with Aran knitting, a number of early garments feature some openwork, either on the center panel or on the side panels. They are attractive and worth considering if a lighter-weight garment is desired. The **Openwork Fan** is a pretty pattern, and because it is worked over a panel of 27 sts, it is ideal as a center panel. Instructions are as follows:
Row 1 (right side): P5, k5, p7, k5, p5.
Row 2 and all wrong-side rows: Purl.
Row 3: P3, p2tog, k2, yo, k1, yo, k2, p2, p3tog, p2, k2, yo, k1, yo, k2, p2tog, p3.

Wishbone Cable.

Row 5: P2, p2tog, k2, yo, k3, yo, k2, p1, p3tog, p1, k2, yo, k3, yo, k2, p2tog, p2.
Row 7: P1, p2tog, k2, yo, k5, yo, k2, p3tog, k2, yo, k5, yo, k2, p2tog, p1.
Row 8: Purl.
Rep rows 1 to 8.

Bobbles are often used for added texture, but do not "overbobble," or you may create too busy (and heavy) an effect. Bobbles are best used at specific points in patterns, e.g., at the center of a diamond, on the center rows of zigzag patterns (see back of child's traditional sweater, page 9), or well spaced on a straight panel of stocking stitch. There are various methods of working bobbles. Here is one of the most popular, worked on 1 st on the right side: K1, yo, k1, yo, k1, into same st; turn and p5; turn and k5; turn and p5; turn and k2togb (k2tog through back loop), k1, k2tog; turn and p3tog; turn, and with yarn in back, slip bobble to right needle (rn).

Irish Knots are smaller and neater, and they require less yarn than bobbles, so they can be used more freely. To make an Irish Knot over 1 st, work as follows: K1, p1, k1, p1, k1, loosely into same stitch; then using point of ln, pass each st (working from left to right) separately over last st. —A.S.

fore been committed to paper. He also employed knitters in the Outer Hebrides of Scotland to knit Aran sweaters for sale.

Kiewe had deeply romantic notions about "the noble and illiterate islander," despite the fact that by the time he had discovered Aran knitting, life on the islands had changed, with communication, education, and emigration playing a more significant role than they previously had. Kiewe was convinced that the patterns were over 1,000 years old and had deep religious significance. He is responsible for having named many of the patterns and having given them religious meaning. For example, to make the Holy Trinity Stitch, also known as Blackberry Stitch, you knit three stitches from one stitch, then one stitch from three stitches, which he claims is directly symbolic of The Father, The Son, and The Holy Ghost. Although his explanations are interesting, I find it impossible to support the view that the Aran knitters had symbolic and mystical purposes in working their patterns. The islanders were, and are, an eminently practical people.

What can positively be said of Aran knitting is that the imagery is that of the Celtic art tradition. The year 250 B.C. is generally agreed upon as marking the start of the invasion of Britain by the the people of the Iron Age known as the Celts. After Britain had been conquered by the Romans, then invaded by the Angles and Saxons in the early centuries A.D., the Celtic language and culture were pushed to the periphery of the country—to Cornwall, Wales, the Isle of Man, Ireland, and Scotland. The Celts' distinctive art consisted of highly complex, mathematically based interlacing and knots. The style began as pagan but reached amazing levels of perfection after the beginning of Christianity. Fortunately, many examples of Celtic Christian art still exist.

The arrival of St. Augustine in Kent in 597 A.D. marks the advent of Roman Christianity in Britain, and following the Synod of Whitby in 663, the Celtic Christian churches were regarded as heretic. This was the beginning of the end for Celtic art, and the years that followed were years of eclipse. This eclipse had been almost total until the revival of interest in Celtic art during the 20th century.

The Celtic language has survived best in the more remote areas, and therefore it is not so strange that, in a remote community with little outside influence, the heritage should express itself in some tangible form. The interlacing and textured effects in Aran knitting bear a remarkable resemblance to Celtic artwork. The Aran Islands are a surviving pocket of Celtic culture where Gaelic is still spoken. But even with these origins firmly established, it is impossible to say whether the Aran knitters began translating this imagery to knitting 100 or 1,000 years ago. Similarly, it is impossible to say whether they had any religious meanings in mind.

Making a traditional Aran sweater

As far as is known, the islanders knit their patterns exclusively into fishing sweaters for their menfolk. Traditional Arans were knit in a thick, undyed (natural cream color) *bainin* yarn. The traditional *bainin* Aran fishing sweater, of which the child's sweater pictured on pages 8 and 9 is an example, has patterns worked in vertical panels. The center panel on the front and back were sometimes different.

The traditional Aran sweater, or "fishing shirt," consists of four separate pieces—a back and a front that are alike and two sleeves. The saddle shoulders, which are worked as a continuation of the center sleeve, give the neck its square shape. The knitter works the collar in circular fashion by picking up the stitches of the back neck, the front neck, and the top of the saddles. The collar depth can vary according to individual taste.

Aran sweaters are worked on two needles in a thick Aran, or *bainin,* yarn, which is slightly heavier than worsted weight, usually with from 70 yd./50 g. to 90 yd./50 g. (approximately 40 yd./oz. to 50 yd./oz.), depending on the brand. Aran-weight yarn is produced by most major spinners in the United Kingdom and is available in many colors. Any wool yarn with a fairly firm twist and a yardage within these figures should give good results. For the average Aran sweater with cable patterns on the front, the back, and the sleeves, you will need about 33% more yarn than for the same size sweater knit in a plain stocking stitch.

If other than the traditional shape is desired, keep the shapes fairly simple in order to accommodate the cable patterns. For example, raglan styling is unsuitable for the traditional allover designs because the sleeve and body shaping cuts into the patterns and produces untidy edges.

Measuring—Draw a diagram of the proposed sweater. Calculate and note on your plan what its exact measurements should be. The measurements needed for a traditional Aran sweater, as shown in the drawing on page 14, are:
A. Body width. This should be one half of the actual chest mea-

This classic Celtic interlacing border is remarkably similar to the Fivefold Aran braid that is shown on page 11 .

surement plus at least 1 in., in order to allow for body movement.

B. Length from shoulder line to lower edge of sweater. Note that the shoulder line is lower than normal because of the saddle insertions. On an adult-size sweater, it is about 2 in. lower.

C. Length from underarm to lower edge.

D. Neck width. On the average it is one-third the body-width measurement (A).

E. Sleeve length.

F. Sleeve width above rib.

G. Sleeve width at top of arm (approximately twice F).

H. Saddle width (approximately 4 in. for an adult size).

Planning and fitting the patterns—The beauty of Aran knitting lies in the form and texture of the patterns, the results of which often have a highly embossed, al-most sculpted appearance. These effects are mainly achieved when the knitter interweaves the stitches with a cable needle. The possibilities and permutations are endless, ranging from simple rope cables to complex interlacing structures. For the knitter, however, complex appearances are often deceiving, as most cable patterns are not difficult to execute.

The front, back, and sleeves of the sweater always have a center pattern panel with narrower pattern panels arranged symmetrically at the sides. There are no rules other than this. The center panel can be any width the knitter wishes. The pattern arrangement on the sleeves need not be the same as on the back and front. When the center panels on the back and front are wide, an arrangement of only the narrower back and front panels often fits better on the sleeves. On some traditional sweaters the center panels on the back and front were different. The choice and arrangement of pattern panels are virtually infinite, allowing the knitter to create a unique design.

Simple knit-and-purl combinations are worked at the edges of the garment's back, front, and sleeves. The edge panels can vary in width according to preference, but it is advisable to work at least a narrow simple panel at the edges to make the seaming neater and to make increasing on sleeves easier. The most popular edge stitch is Moss Stitch, which is worked over an even number of stitches, as follows:

Rows 1 and 2: K1, p1; rep across.
Rows 3 and 4: P1, k1; rep across.

Once you have chosen the pattern panels, be sure to knit up samples of *each* pattern to determine the total number of stitches required for the desired width. It is not possible to accurately calculate the stitches

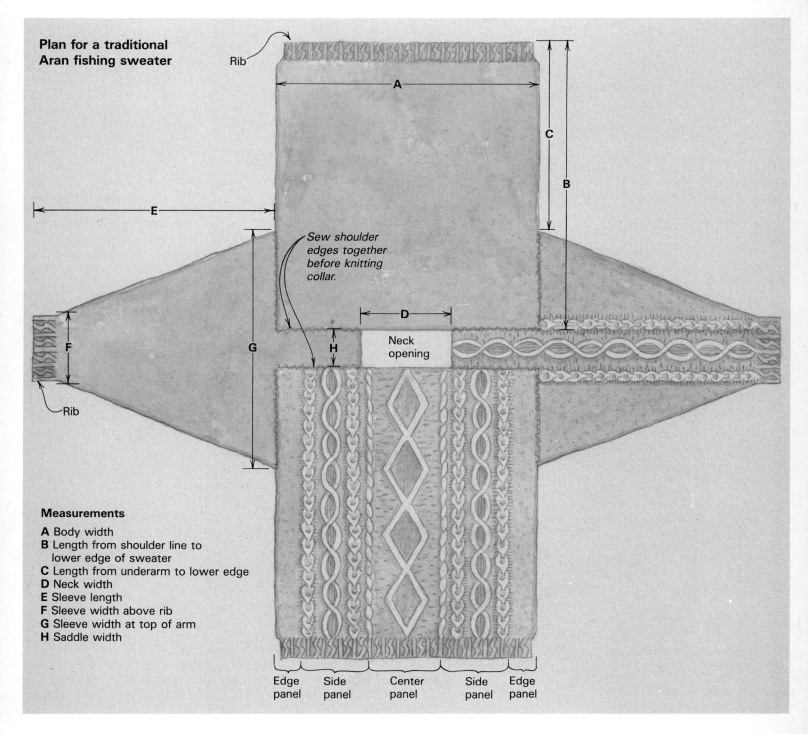

Plan for a traditional Aran fishing sweater

Rib

A

C

B

E

Sew shoulder edges together before knitting collar.

D

G

F

Rib

H

Neck opening

Edge panel | Side panel | Center panel | Side panel | Edge panel

Measurements

A Body width
B Length from shoulder line to lower edge of sweater
C Length from underarm to lower edge
D Neck width
E Sleeve length
F Sleeve width above rib
G Sleeve width at top of arm
H Saddle width

Aran yarns come in a variety of colors today. The garment at left is a contemporary interpretation of an Aran sweater that was inspired by the football jersey. The color and patterns in the above sweater, which is knit in a modern Aran-weight yarn, were inspired by the fishing boats' rusty chains, anchor, and ropes.

required for an Aran by making the usual overall gauge swatch. This is because the pattern panels, depending on their density, contract or expand the work to widely varying degrees. Only by measuring the width of each panel (including the stitches between pattern panels), will you arrive at an accurate figure. Add or subtract stitches in the edge panels as necessary.

Note your chosen patterns, how many times each is to be used, and how many stitches there are in each panel. When you have worked out the final arrangement, total the pattern panel stitches, the stitches between panels, and the edge panel stitches. The result will be the number of stitches required for the desired width.

When you begin to knit the garment, always read the instructions for each pattern panel separately. Do not attempt to write out row-by-row instructions of all the panels together. Because patterns vary in numbers of rows, this is extremely difficult to do. It is also confusing and time-consuming. Concentrate on the first few rows until the patterns are set. Once you see the patterns emerging, you'll soon be able to work without reading the instructions at all.

Working out the ribs—Most traditional sweaters have k2, p2 ribs at the waist and cuffs or patterned ribs of very small cables on a purl ground with knit panels between. The Little Chain Welt, shown in the ribbing of the child's traditional sweater on pages 8 and 9 , is worked as follows, on a multiple of 8 sts plus 2 sts:

Row 1 (right side): *K2, p1, sl1 to cn (cable needle) and hold at front, k1, then k1 from cn (FC [front cross]); sl1 to cn and hold at back, k1, then k1 from cn (BC [back cross]); p1; rep from *, end k2.
Row 2: P2, *k1, p4, k1, p2; rep from *.
Row 3: *K2, p1, BC, FC, p1; rep from *, end k2.
Row 4: Same as row 2.
Rep rows 1 through 4.

For both body and sleeves, the ribs are worked on finer needles, with fewer stitches than the main pieces (about 1 st less for every 8 sts). Make sure the rib pattern fits the total number of rib stitches, adding or subtracting a few stitches as necessary. Once you have worked the rib to the desired length, increase evenly over the next row to the number of stitches required for the body or sleeve piece.

Back and front neck—Work the back and front straight until the desired length to the neck edge is reached. Measure the number of stitches required for the neck width. For the shoulders, cast off the stitches on each side of the centered neck stitches, putting the neck stitches on a holder.

Sleeve shaping—From the top of the rib, the sleeve is gradually and evenly increased at each side. Calculate the number of stitches required for measurements F and G. Subtract F from G to get the total number of stitches to be increased. Divide this total by 2 to get the number of increase rows to be worked (because you will increase 2 sts on each increase row—one at each edge).

Calculate the total number of pattern rows required for the sleeve by measuring and counting the equivalent length on the body. Divide the total number of sleeve rows by the number of increase rows. The result will indicate on which rows to increase. For example, if the total number of sleeve rows is 130 and the number of increase rows is 30, divide 130 by 30 to get 4 plus 10. In other words, increase 1 st at each edge on every 4th row until you have the number of stitches in the G measurement; then work 10 rows straight.

The saddle shoulders are worked as a continuation of the center sleeve, the stitches on each side being cast off. For an adult size the saddle is about 4 in. wide, but this width can be adjusted slightly so the saddle incorporates a complete part of the pattern, becoming an integral part of the design.

The collar—Work the collar after you have sewn up the pieces, as shown in the drawing on the facing page. Using a set of four needles or a small circular needle, pick up all the stitches around the neck, and work the collar even in a rib stitch for as long as you want it. The traditional gansey usually has a deep collar, which is sometimes turned over to the outside. If you want a collar that turns over, and you use a fancy welt pattern, work the pattern on the inside of the collar so the right side will show when the collar is turned over. □

Alice Starmore, of Scotland, is a knit designer, an author, and a knitting instructor. Photos by the author.

Shetland Lace

These intricate shawls mark handknitting's finest hour

by Alice Korach

he moment I saw the old photograph of an exquisite lace shawl from the Shetland isle of Unst, my desire to make and possess its equal was kindled. First I looked up the description and diagram of Shetland shawls in *Mary Thomas's Knitting Book*. From there I turned to Barbara Walker's pattern books and selected an edging that I liked and half a dozen lace patterns. I was an experienced knitter, so most of my choices were 30- to 48-row patterns with very large multiples. My next step was to find the thinnest yarn and needles imaginable—I bought a 1-lb. cone of 30/1 unbleached linen and three sets of size 0 circular needles.

I was ready to make my treasure, I thought, but first I decided to knit up some samples. This was the smartest thing I had done thus far. While knitting my samples, I discovered that complex patterns are a nightmare, especially for a person who has never knit any lace patterns. Fortunately, complexity doesn't really suit the style of Shetland lace anyway; its essence is simplicity. So I selected simpler patterns and practiced knitting swatches of each until I felt reasonably comfortable.

The other nightmare, which I decided to live with, was the fiber. Linen is beautiful, but a yarn that has no stretch and great stiffness is absurd for a first project, especially when gossamer-weight wool is readily available and inexpensive. After selecting patterns and measuring my gauge, I calculated multiples, stitch numbers, and repeats; wrote it all down; and started knitting. Two years later, with many other projects intervening, I blocked my linen shawl (behind the model on the cover). It is nowhere near the equal of the shawl that inspired me, but as I have gained more experience with lace, I have also gained the certainty that I will eventually design and knit something that splendid. Patience and perseverance are all.

If you want to knit lace desperately enough, you can learn to do it, even if you are not an expert knitter. The only stitches required to knit lace are knit, purl, slip, yarn over, and two or three types of decreases, but your tension must be even and loose. If your stockinette knitting is puckered or stiff, lace is probably beyond you right now—keep working at knitting smoothly. Once you've mastered that, you'll be able to knit Shetland lace. Be patient, get comfortable with the yarn and needles, keep it simple, knit swatches, calculate multiples carefully, count accurately, and, above all, keep at it.

This sampler handkerchief includes all of the patterns considered authentic by Mary Thomas. Print o' the Wave appears in the center. Clockwise from the top are: Ears o' Grain, Razor Shell, Bird's Eye, Horseshoe, Fern, Old Shale, Acre (checkered and ploughed), Cat's Paw, and Fir Cone.

The traditional shawl—Unst-style lace is produced from the finest possible handspun wool. There are only a few spinners who are even capable of spinning a woolen thread two to four hairs thick and then plying two of the threads together. The knitting must be done very carefully and loosely so that the fragile yarn does not break. When it is completed, a 6-ft. shawl weighs as little as 2 oz., is knit of two to three miles of yarn, and can be drawn through a wedding ring—hence the name ring shawl. The spinning and the knitting of a large shawl might each take as long as one year.

The classic shawl was most often knit of creamy-white natural yarn; although buff, gray, and dark natural wools were also popular. Many lace shawls were knit in black and purple during the 19th century, when these were the colors of mourning. Red stripes or borders were popular for celebratory use, and Sarah Don prints a picture of a magnificent red-and-cream-striped wedding veil in her book, *The Art of Shetland Lace* (see "Resources," page 20). All varieties of striping and shading in almost any color are authentic. Nevertheless, because the lace patterns themselves appear so intricate, too much color can detract from their gossamer perfection. Besides, since the finest commercial yarn comes in white only, you'll have to dye your own colors.

Shetland lace shawls are usually square and perfectly symmetrical, although beautiful examples exist that are triangular, round, or oblong, and some even have cap-shaped tops. In fact, all sorts of garments can be knit in Shetland lace patterns—stockings, gloves, capes, christening robes, and wedding veils—but the square form is the classical one for the laciest work. Perhaps this is so because of the extreme blocking required to finish the piece to best effect. When a lace shawl is correctly stretched, it becomes almost one third larger, and all the holes created by the yarn-over/decrease combinations open to reveal the patterns.

Mary Thomas writes that there are only ten authentic Shetland lace patterns, all of which are images of natural things (ferns, fir cones, shale, etc.), as can be seen in the handkerchief sampler on the facing page. This seems unlikely. Thomas wrote during a period when romantic theories were popularly ascribed to traditional British crafts. Sarah Don draws the obvious conclusion that individual knitters can work these few patterns in countless ways and recombine them endlessly. A knitter can easily invent his or her own patterns either accidentally or purposely. Pictures of museum pieces collected from Shetland knitters at the turn of the century reveal numerous patterns that are not listed in *Mary Thomas's Knitting Book*. Barbara Walker's three volumes of patterns (see "Resources," page 20) show the enormous variety of lace shapes from all over the world, many of which are extremely complex.

One thing that distinguishes Shetland patterns is that no difficult techniques are employed. Although complex in design, Shetland lace was a relatively easy knitting technique to pass along from mother to daughter. The work is also simplified by a frequently used technique, whereby there is no definite right side, as the stitches are worked in garter, rather than stockinette stitch. With the very fine yarn used in traditional lace, the bumpiness of garter stitch is not obtrusive. But generally, today's commercially available two-ply lace-weight yarn appears smoother when knit with a right side. This is up to the knitter's aesthetic sense, and it is one reason knitters can produce such strikingly different results from the same pattern.

Construction—A square shawl is worked with no bound-off edges and with a minimum of casting on. The sequence, which is shown on page 19, is to knit one edge lengthwise, pick up the inside edge, and knit from it one border and the center in one piece. The remaining three border pieces are grafted to the center, either invisibly or in such a way as to produce lace holes. As a result, there are no thick or rigid sections, and a fine shawl really can pass through a ring.

Start a shawl by knitting a scalloped edging to the desired length of one side, but remember that blocking will stretch the work by nearly one third. Put the last row of stitches on a pin or very small holder and pick up along the long, straight inner edge the number of stitches needed for the border, often every second stitch. Then knit these stitches to the desired height, forming the multipatterned, mitered border. Knit the first third of the border on the total number of stitches; knit the remaining two thirds of the border, decreasing one stitch at the end of every row. Work a row of holes as the last row of the first border by alternating k2tog and yo. The central square is usually set off with a row or two of plain knitting and is then knit directly above the holes. Leave the work on a spare needle when you're finished.

Knit the second, third, and fourth edges and border combinations to the exact specifications of the first edge, omitting the row of holes. You will create the holes on these three sides by grafting in a simple manner: lacing the grafting thread through two stitches from the center and two stitches from the border. Before grafting the side borders, pick up evenly, on spare needles, the appropriate number of stitches along each side of the square. The grafting must be kept very loose, as shown in the left-hand photo on page 18, to allow the shawl its full stretch. If you prefer a grafted finish that looks like right-side knitting, as you might if you're using a heavier yarn, knit holes into each of the border sections, and then graft right sides up, maintaining the same tension so that the graft will be

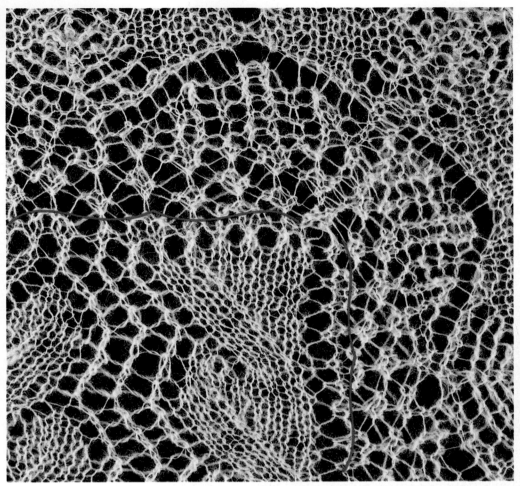

Tension the grafting stitches, marked by red bracket at right side of cable motif, to approximate the size of the knit holes, which are bracketed above the motif.

Shetland lace looks uninspiring as it is being knit (above). It must be stretched out so that the stitches can be seen (right), and when finished, the piece must be blocked so that its full glory is revealed.

A Shetland lace wedding handkerchief

Gauge: If your gauge is approximately 12 rows and 6 sts to the inch, stretched, on 0000 needles with gossamer-weight Shetland wool, the handkerchief will block to 23 in. square. It requires just under 1 oz. of wool. For more on gauge and lace, see "Choosing patterns," facing page.

Construct as follows:

1. *Edge* (218 rows): Loosely cast on 12 sts by holding both needles together and casting onto them as if they were one needle. Slide the extra needle out of the loops to start knitting. Knit 27 repeats of Cyprus Edging, plus 2 rows. Break off the yarn, leaving a tail 3 in. to 5 in. long, and place the stitches on a safety pin.

2. *Border* (52 rows in garter stitch): Starting at the cast-on end, which puts the ridge on the right side, pick up 109 sts in the loops along the flat edge of the Cyprus Edging. This means picking up a stitch for every other row. Pick up the loops, not the long horizontal stitches, to make the join almost invisible. Leaving a tail, knit 2 plain rows. Knit 10 rows of bead stitch, followed by 1 plain row. Knit the first 5 rows of the center border pattern on the 109 sts. Starting with the 6th row, for the rest of the border, decrease 1 st at the end of every row (34 decreases will leave 75 sts). These 34 rows will be the 23 remaining rows of the center border pattern, 1 plain row above it, 8 rows of bead stitch, and 2 plain rows.

3. *Center* (132 rows): Above the last 2 plain rows, knit 1 row of holes on the remaining 75 sts as follows: K1, *O, T* to the end. Print o' the Wave (center panel) has a definite right side. Purl 1 row, and then follow the pattern (3 repeats across) 8 times, plus 2 rows (130 rows). Leave these stitches on the needle and secure them by wrapping a rubber band around the point. Break off the yarn, leaving a tail.

4. Repeat steps 1 and 2. Graft the 75 sts at the end of step 2 to the 75 sts at the end of step 3 so the center square has a border at the top and bottom: Hold the center nearest you and remove the band from the end of the needle that corresponds to the open end of the border needle. Make sure the ridges (purls) along the top of each scalloped edge are on the same side. You can graft on the right or wrong side, but be consistent. Use a blunt-point tapestry needle for grafting and a 4-ft. to 5-ft. tail of yarn. Lace through 1 st on the center and 1 st on the border, leaving a tail to weave in later. For the rest of the graft, lace through 2 sts at a time on the center and border alternately to form holes. Don't lace tightly; allow room for the holes, and stretch.

5, 6. To form the borders for the remaining two sides, repeat step 4 twice and pick up 75 sts evenly along each side of the center to graft onto.

7. *Mitered corners:* With one knitting needle on each side of a corner, pick up stitches, starting at the center: 13 to the top wave, 16 to the lower wave, 9 to the edge, 11 along the cast-on of the edge to correspond to the 11 on the safety pin. Using the tapestry needle and a piece of 2-ft. yarn, lace through 1 st at a time on each side of the corner; leave a tail at each end to weave in. Make sure the pattern edges match perfectly, and pick up different stitches as necessary to ensure a good match. Allow enough yarn in the graft for stretch.

8. Weave all ends securely into the back and clip off excess thread.

9. *Finishing:* Use four straight pins and a spool of colored thread to lay out a 23-in. square on a bed or sheet-covered carpet. Wash the work in Ivory flakes and tepid water; rinse well. Starting 1 in. to 2 in. from a corner, pin it along one thread side, piercing the tip of each scallop. Stretch each side straight in the same way, but less than 23 in. Then stretch them once or twice more until they won't stretch further. Dry 24 hours. —A.K.

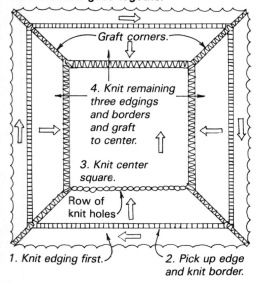

How a shawl goes together

Graft corners.

4. Knit remaining three edgings and borders and graft to center.

3. Knit center square.

Row of knit holes

1. Knit edging first.

2. Pick up edge and knit border.

invisible. Finally, weave the ends into the back of the shawl.

When grafting the corners, measure the diagonal opening and pick up the appropriate number of stitches per inch, as in your gauge. One set of edge stitches will be on a stitch holder; the other must be picked up from the loosely cast-on edge. Getting the patterns to match at the miter is tricky, but dropping or adding a few stitches on one side or the other can do it. By the fourth border, the work flies. Besides, with all the holes and stretch, there aren't nearly as many stitches as you might assume.

Contemporary tools and materials—Very fine lace is usually knit on 000 or 0000 needles (1.5mm-1.25mm in diameter), called "wires" by the Scottish knitters. Finding these needles is a serious problem for the American knitter who wants to produce a large piece of cobweb lace, since the longest extra-fine needles I've been able to find domestically are only 8 in., and circular needles don't come smaller than 0. For the real thing, see Scottish suppliers under "Resources," page 20.

If you don't want to wait to hear from Scotland, you can use 8-in. 000 or 0000 needles to make an heirloom, framable wedding handerchief, as described in the box below. These double-pointed German needles are extremely sharp. To protect yourself from punctures and prevent your knitting from sliding off, wrap a small rubber band around the base of each needle, but don't leave the bands on between projects, as they can damage the metal's finish.

Silk, linen, and fine cotton produce magnificent lace, but they present certain problems that lovely, soft, stretchy wool doesn't. They don't stretch, which makes it harder to maintain an even gauge. Being less hairy, they are liable to slip off the needle without warning. Finally, fine silk fuzzes if your skin is the least bit rough. Your pharmacist can recommend a nongreasy hand cream, such as Carmol 10, which you must use religiously. Even with wool it's wise to use the cream to prevent the yarn's snagging on winter-roughened hands.

Choosing patterns—No matter what patterns you select, always knit samples. Not only will samples help you determine gauge (height in rows to width in stitches—*after* blocking), which is essential if you intend to produce a square shawl or handerchief, but they'll also help you find, and perhaps fix, flawed patterns.

Gauge is a more flexible concept in lace knitting than in garment knitting. Because the lace stretches a lot, and since some parts are usually more dense than others, the gauge is somewhat variable. To design a shawl with a square center, you must have a reasonable approximation of the stretched gauge for the center pattern and the border patterns. The figures may not be the same, but you have to know how

---

Cyprus Edging
(Cast on 12.)
1. S, K5, T, O, K1, T, K1.
2. K4, O, T, K2, O, T, K1.
3. S, K3, T, O, K1, T, K2.
4. K7, O, T, K1.
5. S, K4, O, T, K1, O,O, K2.
6. K2, K1, P1, K2, O, K3, O, T, K1.
7. S, K6, O, T, K4.
8. Bind off 2, K2, O, K5, O, T, K1.

Print o' the Wave for center square
(Multiple of 24 + 3)
1. K4 *T, K3, [O,T] 3x, O, K13* end K12.
2. P all even rows.
3. K3* T, K3, O, K1, O [SKP, O] 3x, K3, SKP, K7*.
5. K2* T, [K3,O] 2x, [SKP, O] 3x, K3, SKP, K5* end K6.
7. K1* T, K3, O, K5, O [SKP, O] 3x, K3, SKP, K3* end K5.
9. *K12, O, [SKP, O] 3x, K3, SKP, K1* end K4.
11. *K7, T, K3, [O, T] 3x, O, K1, O, K3, SKP* end K3.
13. K6* T, K3, [O,T] 3x, [O, K3] 2x, SKP, K5* end K2.
15. K5* T, K3, [O,T] 3x, O, K5, O, K3, SKP, K3* end K1.
16. P.

This gossamer-wool handkerchief has large waves opposite one another filled with the Spiderweb pattern. Knitted in mohair on size 11-15 needles, this would make a shawl.

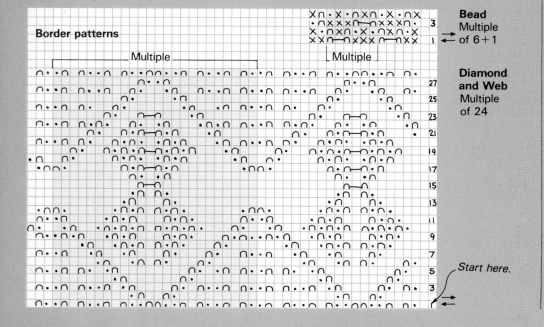

Border patterns

Multiple · · · · · · · · Multiple

Bead
Multiple of 6+1

Diamond and Web
Multiple of 24

Start here.

Key to symbols

Written	Charted	
K	⊠	Knit
P	⊡	Purl
O	∩	Yarn over
T	·	K2tog
SKP	∪	Sl, k1, psso
STP	—	Sl, k2tog, psso
S		Sl st knitwise
*		Repeat from asterisk
[ ] 3x		Repeat what's in brackets 3x

many rows it will take to make the center square and how many stitches the border needs to match it. Some fudging will probably be necessary, and careful stretching of the finished piece can make up for any remaining inconsistencies.

Occasionally pattern instructions make more sense when written out than when charted, but I usually prefer charted patterns, like those described on page 19, as they show how the stitches and rows lie in relation to each other. In fact, I didn't understand lace and couldn't have designed my own until I learned to convert written patterns to charts. It's very logical, and the instructions in Barbara Walker's *Charted Knitting Designs* make it easy to learn.

Charts help me stay in pattern during decreases, especially when yarn overs come near the edge, and I find them invaluable when I have to figure out faulty directions. Charts are particularly useful for locating the center of a shape to ensure symmetry. Remember that a chart must be read right to left and then left to right, or vice versa. Each row does *not* begin at the same edge of the chart.

You can limit yourself to the ten classic patterns, or you can let your imagination run wild. However, if you want to produce a work of art that is symmetrical in all respects, be careful to choose neighboring patterns that have the same multiple or that are multiples of each other. For example, you can plan a border with patterns that repeat over 5 sts, 10 sts, or 20 sts, such that several of one pattern will fit exactly above or below one of another. This will satisfy the eye, will be easy to remember, and will allow your corner patterns to miter perfectly. I planned the border of my wool shawl this way.

A different, but satisfying, approach that allows the greatest creative latitude is to place a smaller pattern, like a tree, above, below, or between the same part of a long wave or diamond pattern and to fill between with plain knitting or perhaps a diamond of bird's eyes or spiders. The border of the handkerchief whose pattern accompanies this article uses that principle.

You can knit the central square in garter stitch, as Mary Thomas says is traditional for Shetland shawls; in a single lacy pattern, like my wool prize-winner, worn by the model on the cover; or in stripes of complex and numerically complementary patterns, like the magnificent 19th-century Unst shawls. I often choose patterns that symbolize the use or the intended owner of the piece. For example, in a wedding handkerchief, I prefer mostly female and fertility images, which might include water, webs, strawberries, and nets. Do what you like. Just make it square according to your gauge. You should also consider whether your swatch stretches more lengthwise or widthwise. You might have to compensate by knitting the piece a little wider or longer than square.

Tips on lace knitting—Here are a few tips and reminders that will help you when you're ready to pick up your needles to try lace knitting.

• Hold thin needles gently to keep the tension loose and even and to prevent your hands from cramping.

• To ensure even distribution of stitches when picking them up along edging or sides, mark the length in fourths with safety pins.

• When you knit the row after a double yarn over, knit the first over, and purl the second each time. Double-overs make large holes.

• Yarn overs and togethers tend to cross on the left-hand needle. Be very careful to knit the stitches in their proper order.

• When decreasing, make sure that you don't inadvertently drop a stitch, and check to see that you've decreased the correct number of stitches. If the row ends with an over/decrease combination, you may have to do a double decrease, or you can omit the over. Choose the neatest alternative.

• Corner grafts are tricky. Keep a careful count of the stitches you pick up in relation to their position on the pattern. Be prepared to make slight adjustments.

• When you have completed and grafted your last border, you are ready to wash and block your masterpiece. Wash it gently in tepid water, using a mild soap like Ivory flakes. Don't use detergent and don't wring or vigorously agitate it, as heat and rough treatment will cause the wool to felt. Rinse the shawl thoroughly, and remove excess water by rolling it in a towel.

• Stretch the shawl on a king-size mattress pad or on a clean sheet pinned to a carpet that's out of traffic. When you stretch the shawl, the sheet will be subject to a considerable amount of pull, so try to keep it flat. Use straight pins and thread to outline a square the size the shawl should become. Start pinning through the tip of each scallop at opposite corners. Don't stretch the shawl to its full size all at once. Pin it out smaller. Then gradually stretch it as far as it will go. If it dries too fast, mist it with water in a spray bottle. The shawl may turn out a little smaller or larger than you expected, but it should definitely be square. Let it dry completely before you unpin it. If sections contract when it's unpinned, then it's still wet. You'll have to reblock each time you wash the shawl, but you shouldn't have to do that very often.

I can't begin to tell you the satisfaction and pride you'll feel as you unpin your first Shetland lace shawl. At last you can see the shawl with all its holes fully and equally open, and you know that you are an artist. You have created your first knitted-lace masterpiece. The next one will be even more beautiful. □

Alice Korach is a part-time English professor and a full-time knitter, spinner, and weaver. She has been knitting since she was eight and for the last ten years has concentrated on original designs.

Resources

Books

Compton, Rae. *The Complete Book of Traditional Knitting.* New York: Charles Scribner's Sons, 1983. *This book has a good selection of patterns, especially of pointed edgings.*

Don, Sarah. *The Art of Shetland Lace.* London: Bell & Hyman Ltd., 1981. *This is a classic, with good pictures and background information. Many patterns have errors, however, so you must test them carefully.*

Thomas, Mary. *Mary Thomas's Knitting Book.* New York: Dover Publications, 1972 (originally published in 1938).

Thomas, Mary. *Mary Thomas's Book of Knitting Patterns.* New York: Dover Publications, 1972 (originally published in 1943).

Walker, Barbara G. *A Treasury of Knitting Patterns.* New York: Charles Scribner's Sons, 1968.

Walker, Barbara G. *A Second Treasury of Knitting Patterns.* New York: Charles Scribner's Sons, 1970.

Walker, Barbara G. *Charted Knitting Designs: A Treasury of Knitting Patterns.* New York: Charles Scribner's Sons, 1982. *All of Barbara Walker's books are superb sources. I haven't encountered a flawed pattern in any of them. This is the only volume that contains charted patterns, but it has good directions for converting to charts.*

Supplies

Beggars' Lace
Box 17263
Denver, CO 80217
(303) 722-5557
8-in. needles and nonwool fibers.

Lacis
2982 Adeline St.
Berkeley, CA 94703
(415) 843-7178
8-in. needles and nonwool fibers.

Elizabeth Zimmermann
6899 Cary Bluff
Pittsville, WI 54466
(715) 884-2799
Only domestic source for gossamer-weight Shetland wool (Shetland Cobweb); 8-in. needles in four sizes; all the lace-knitting books listed above.

Anderson and Co.
Shetland Warehouse
6062 Commercial St.
Lerwick, Shetland, Scotland, ZE1 OBD
011-44-595-3714
Shawl-length knitting needles 0, 00, and 000, their sizes 14, 15, and 16. Available by mail; VISA accepted.

Jamieson & Smith
Shetland Wool Brokers, Ltd.
90 North Road
Lerwick, Shetland, Scotland ZE1 0PQ
011-44-595-3579
Shetland yarns, from gossamer weight up. Skeins and free samples available by mail.

Exploring a Knitted Pattern

Bohus Stickning sweater generates diverse designs knit with simple stitches

by Margaret Bruzelius

One of my fondest childhood memories is of my grandmother at family feasts, dressed in her usual "grandma" clothes, except for a beautiful pale gray cardigan with a yoke patterned in blues and greens. Year after year, this cardigan was brought out for celebrations. Then it was carefully folded in tissue paper and preserved in mothballs in the bottom drawer, among her other "best" clothes. But this sweater, along with the pride and love with which my grandmother wore it, is the only garment she owned that remains vivid in my mind.

The cardigan, still folded in tissue and redolent of mothballs, was given to me on my grandmother's death, and for many years it lay in my bottom drawer, taken out, as before, only on ceremonial occasions. When I began to design knitting patterns, I decided to find out more about it and study its intricate patterns. In the process, my original love for it was augmented by admiration for the imagination and workmanship lavished on it.

A history of Bohus Stickning—My mother bought the cardigan in Stockholm in 1948. It was produced by Bohus Stickning, a small hand-knitting business started in the late 1930s by Emma Jacobsson, the wife of the governor of Bohus Province in southern Sweden. The business was begun to provide relief work for the wives of unemployed stonecutters, and after a few false starts making Christmas ornaments and stuffed animals, it settled on knitting unadorned socks and mittens. Soon, encouraged by the stores to which she supplied these knits, Emma Jacobsson began to design patterned sweaters. When her source for Finnish yarn dried up because of the war, she encouraged local farmers to supply wool; this wool was spun and dyed to Bohus's specifications. Eventually, these yarns were supplemented by fine angoras spun in Italy. Bohus knitters were trained to a remarkable level of proficiency, and

the business expanded to include other designers, eventually employing six in all.

The province of Bohus, unlike other parts of Scandinavia, had no surviving indigenous knitting tradition. Thus, Emma Jacobsson and her designers used folk motifs from other southern Swedish textiles as their sources, avoiding patterns that were in any way reminiscent of other Scandinavian knitting traditions. Bohus became best known for circular-knit pullovers with patterned yokes, such as those made in Iceland. But Icelandic sweaters have always been heavy, outdoor sweaters, while Bohus sweaters were deliberately much more refined in detail and lighter in weight. Each designer had an individual style, and there seems to have been no effort to develop one particular style, although the patterning on my cardigan (top photo, page 23), as well as that on the hat and sweaters on page 36, is the type for which Bohus is most famous.

From the start, Bohus was devoted to the well-being of its workers. The knitters, who were recruited through classes taught by Bohus teachers, formed a cell and selected one member to be the contact with headquarters. This woman supervised the distribution of yarn and patterns and collected the finished goods. Once a month the knitters met for a tea, paid for by Bohus, at their group leader's home. They were periodically instructed in new techniques and patterns. For many of these rural women, knitting for Bohus presented their first opportunity to earn money, and the monthly meetings were a welcome addition to their limited social life. Their interest in the business and their closeness to it were integral to Bohus's success. Even among women for whom there were few employment opportunities, only a special kind of person would be willing to master the skills necessary to knit sweaters with gauges from 10 to 12 stitches/in. and many color changes.

Unfortunately, as Bohus Province became more prosperous and farmers moved off

the land, fewer and fewer women were willing to continue working for the relatively small wage Bohus could pay them. Factory work became an option outside the home, and television an enticement within it. Bohus could not compete. Moreover, Emma Jacobsson wanted to retire, and the company couldn't find anyone to replace her. Bohus Stickning was dissolved in 1969, leaving behind a legacy of wonderfully vivid design and exquisite craftsmanship.

Analyzing the pattern—When I began to analyze my cardigan, I wanted to imitate the dense, subtle patterning characteristic of Bohus. This is created primarily through an extravagant use of color—Bohus patterns use up to 13 colors. Purl stitches on the face of the fabric create two parallel, broken lines of color and increase the intricacy of the color patterning. The color variations are accentuated by the depth and shadow in the fabric's bumpy surface. Slipped stitches distort the knit rows, increasing the fabric's textural interest.

Though the patterning is complex, Bohus technique builds on the most basic of knitting techniques. Stitches are either worked or slipped, and worked stitches are either knitted or purled. There are no fancy looped stitches or yarn-overs or any of the more ingenious knitting maneuvers.

To recreate my sweater's pattern, I simply assigned letters to each color and wrote in a chart what I thought happened in each row. What a task! The gauge is about 11 stitches to the inch, and the angora yarns have felted with washing so that the stitches are indistinct. A magnifying glass only clarified the fuzz. Finally I isolated a 10-stitch repeat of 68 rows of pattern, with no row repeats at all. I then assigned my own colors to the chart and began to knit.

Problems appeared immediately—there were three or four colors in the same row, which made knitting very tedious, and when I had to pick up a color again, it was invariably at the wrong end of the row. After

*Two Bohus Stickning sweaters and a hat,
courtesy of Elizabeth Zimmerman.*

about 30 rows I gave up. But I continued to think about the pattern, convinced that there must be certain rules governing Bohus patterns, or even their excellent knitters would have gone mad.

I discovered they never used more than two colors in a row; to create the impression of more colors, they used slip stitches. For example, if while you're knitting a red row, you slip stitches from the blue row below, your red row will appear to be knit in both red and blue. Also, Bohus became famous early on for circular pullovers, so even patterns that were knit back and forth probably used circular techniques. Thus, my cardigan must have been knit on double-pointed needles or back and forth on circular needles, and then, if it was necessary to pick up a color at the wrong end of the row, the work could be pushed to the other end of the needle and a second row worked in the same direction. (Of course, in circular garments this would not have been necessary, because every row is worked in the same direction.) I'm sure they were also absolutely fearless and never thought that *anything* was too complicated.

Although I abandoned my attempt to re-create exactly the pattern on my grandmother's sweater, I have continued to explore its elements in numerous patterns of my own. What follows is a group of swatches based on my interpretation of Bohus. I've used a great many yarn types and some very un-Bohus colors, as I feel that there is no point in trying to imitate the designs exactly. The Bohus knitters allowed themselves remarkable freedom. If we learn to be as free in our knitting as they were in theirs, we will have learned a great deal.

Reworking a Bohus pattern—The first two swatches are knit with the simplest Bohus techniques—slip stitches and two-color purl bumps. In the first swatch, "Dotted Squares" (center photo), the first and fifth stitches, which are never worked in blue, form ridges that the blue squares sink between, creating a three-dimensional effect. As I looked at this swatch, it began to resemble toothy mouths, so I reknit it in white and red, eliminating the stitches that formed ridges and slipping some of the white stitches on the white rows to help pull the mouths open ("Cannibal King," bottom photo). If, instead of working only two red rows at a time, you worked six or eight (still slipping the white stitches), you might get the effect of toothy mouths with their tongues hanging out. In these patterns only one color is used per row, and all unworked stitches are slipped purlwise.

The second group has a more typical Bohus motif but uses atypical yarns: pearl cotton and metallic. For the first version, "Carmen Miranda" (top photo, page 24), I spent some time developing exactly the color look that I wanted. In my first attempt, the central, nonrepeating color line in blue did not show up particularly well,

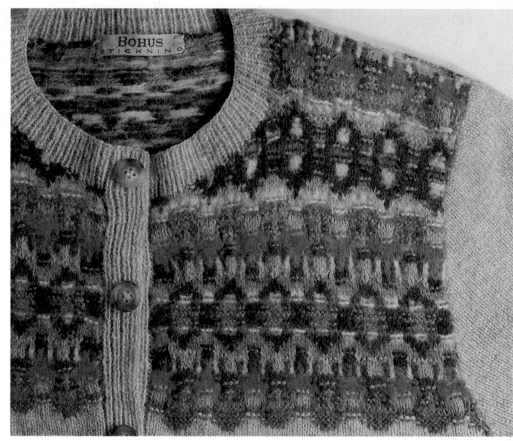

From the richly patterned yoke of the sweater she inherited from her grandmother (above), Bruzelius derived the swatches on this page and pages 24 and 25.

Reading the charts
The charts are read from bottom right to top left. Purl stitches are indicated by a dot in the box; knit stitches are unmarked. Slip stitches are marked with a vertical line and are slipped purlwise. An arrow on the right-hand side means push the work to the other end of the needle and work that row starting from the other end in order to pick up a yarn color at the wrong end of the row. This requires you to work either two right-side or two wrong-side rows consecutively. Double-pointed or circular needles are needed for any pattern where this occurs.

Dotted Squares
Repeat: 8 sts,
8 rows

Cannibal King
Repeat: 8 sts,
12 rows

Before beginning pattern, work two preparation rows in white.

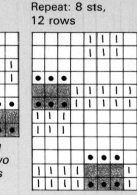

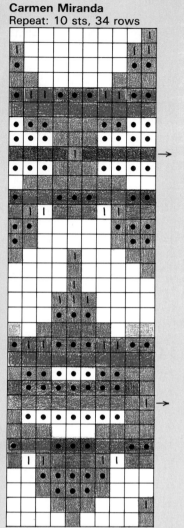

Carmen Miranda
Repeat: 10 sts, 34 rows

"Carmen Miranda" contains a typical Bohus motif but is knit in atypical yarns: pearl cotton and metallic.

By changing the colors of the silk/wool yarns in the two swatches at right, Bruzelius created two different versions of the same pattern: "Spinning Tops I" (near right) and "Spinning Tops II" (far right).

By changing the colors of the silk/wool yarns in the two swatches at right, Bruzelius created two different versions of the same pattern: "Spinning Tops I" (near right) and "Spinning Tops II" (far right).

Spinning Tops
Repeat: 10 sts, 16 rows

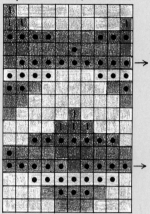

so I changed to red metallic. I liked this but still felt that it could be improved, so I tried blue metallic. This turned out to be my favorite color combination, though Carmen herself might well have preferred the one with red.

In a more subdued vein, I recreated the sweater's upper diamond motif. The first version, "Upper Diamond I" (left photo, below), uses three colors of flat wool yarn, and the second, "Upper Diamond II" (right photo, below), combines flat wool yarn and kid mohair, which is a soft, fine-quality mohair from kid goats. In the first version the motif stands against a strong two-color background, which adds richness to what

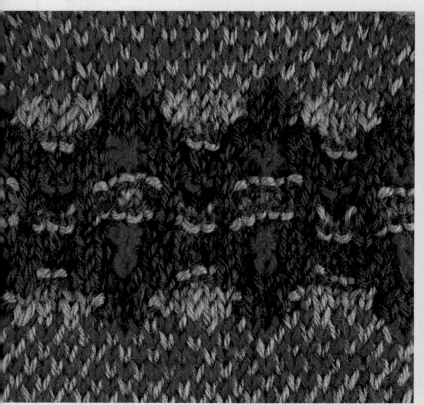

"Upper Diamond I" (left) and "Upper Diamond II" (right) are derived from the olive-green diamond motif at the top of Bruzelius's sweater (page 23).

could otherwise be a rather dull setting for these jewellike patterns.

Working out the mechanics of these patterns irritated me so much that I decided to try a simple all-over pattern, using lots of slip stitches in every row. As a result, I created a dense-looking pattern that is actually simple to work. This was so satisfying that I developed a more complicated all-over pattern from the very bottom section of my sweater's yoke. The next two swatches, "Spinning Tops," I and II (photos above), are the same pattern worked in different weights and colors of silk/wool yarns. In the first version, the pattern's pink central line blends in; in the second version,

the yellow central line stands out. Both are lovely and satisfying to work.

Then I had a wonderful silk tape I wanted to try. After a few unsuccessful attempts, I worked it in a two-color seed-stitch pattern separated by stripes (photo below). Called "Stripe," it may seem too simple to be a Bohus pattern, but it has the same elegance of color as Bohus patterns and, like them, uses the yarn to best advantage. This last swatch sums up my experience reworking my Bohus pattern. Although Bohus patterns seem intimidating because of their intricacy and fine gauge, the principles on which they are based can be used to create wonderful patterns in any yarn,

at any gauge. I worked my swatches on needles from size 3 to size 13. Even the simplest Bohus idea—purling one color above another—can add excitement to a basic striped pattern.

What we learn from looking at the Bohus designers' work is their respect and love for their materials and their craft. They didn't try to force themselves into paths that didn't suit them, but rose to each challenge in their work with imagination and courage. They took the time to think, to teach, and to learn. □

Margaret Bruzelius designs hand knits from her home in Brooklyn, NY.

Upper Diamond
Repeat: 10 sts, 21 rows

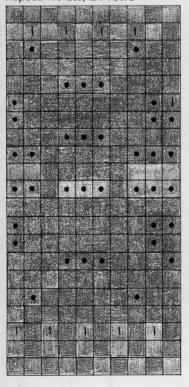

Stripe
Repeat: 2 sts, 20 rows

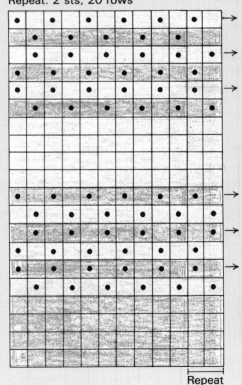

Repeat

Worked in a two-color seed-stitch pattern in silk tape, "Stripe" has all the elegance of traditional Bohus Stickning designs.

Colorful Tvåändsstickning

No matter how you knit in the strands, there are no floats in this dense fabric

by Linda D. Y. Sokalski

tvåändsstickning (Swedish two-strand knitting) is best known for its textured patterns. These patterns are generally worked in white-on-white. Alternate stitches are knit with strands from opposite ends of one ball of yarn, and the yarns are twisted after each stitch (see the article on pp. 50-54). But the wonderful pieces I saw in Swedish museums showed that beautiful color patterns and elaborate embroidery were also commonly used to embellish this unique form of knitting.

On the front side of the work, multicolor *tvåändsstickning* differs little in appearance from Fair Isle knitting or stranded knitting. The reverse side, however, is a different story (see photo, facing page). There are no floats, since the yarns are twisted at least every other stitch, producing a durable, air-tight fabric.

Knitting in colors

I've found the greatest variety of patterns and techniques in mittens and gloves. Even those primarily embellished with textured patterns often have a small amount of color, typically a bit of red on a predominantly white ground. It's common to use one strand of red and one strand of white for either the cast-on or the first row of knitting, which results in a candy-stripe effect on the edge of the work. If two colors are used for the cast-on, the first row is the dividing row (where the stitches are divided evenly onto four needles, a right-side row). If the cast-on is done in a single color with a two-color row following, the work is divided on the second row so that the decorative ridge will appear on the right side. And if the edge incorporates a contrasting color, it's usually used elsewhere in the mitten for balance—often as a pattern in the border.

Multicolor *tvåändsstickning* has no strict rules. A variety of techniques may be used, depending on the type of pattern and the preference of the knitter. But since patterns fall into three categories, there are three distinct techniques. Sometimes more than one of these techniques are used in a single garment.

In allover patterns with two colors, where the colors are used approximately evenly, like the socks in the photo on the facing page, the contrasting color replaces one strand of the background color, and a half-twist occurs at each color change, as in single-color *tvåändsstickning*. In addition, however, the unused color is never allowed to span more than 2 sts of the color being worked. After every 2 sts in one color, the strands are given a full twist. Since it's best to avoid twisting at the same point on subsequent rounds, work out ahead of time the points where the strands are twisted. Some knitters avoid this problem by twisting after every stitch, but the contrasting color tends to show through the front more with this method. Whether you twist every stitch or every other stitch is a matter of taste, but no float should ever be longer than 2 sts. You can avoid the problem of having two balls tangling by winding a single ball with the light color inside and the dark color on the outside.

If the two-color pattern covers only a few rows, and the rest of the garment is one color, you can break one strand of the main color and replace it with the contrasting color for the duration of the pattern. But when there are rows of solid color between pattern rows, as on the socks, many knitters prefer to carry the contrasting color as the second strand, twisting it every stitch or every other stitch, even though it isn't used. This results in a neat, consistent appearance on the reverse side; and the stitches on the front look flatter, more like stockinette, since they're all formed with a single strand of yarn.

You can add a third or even a fourth color, but don't overdo it. You must twist before every stitch, generally around the yarn that would have the longest float, and with four or five strands involved, the work becomes very thick. Also, the many strands become messy, and you must untwist them often.

Isolated motifs scattered in a dominant ground are knit with three strands throughout and are characteristic of the folk costume of Gagnef Parish, in which black snowflake designs are scattered on a solid-red field (sleeve photo below). Two strands of the ground color are used along with a separate ball for the contrasting color

This knit sleeve (detail of a Gagnef folk costume) is worked with two strands of red and one strand of black throughout for the border patterns and snowflakes scattered above them.

Two methods of knitting with colors: The border rounds of the mitten were done with the allover technique, which uses one strand of each color, but the pattern on the back of the hand is a modified intarsia. A strand of red is added for each vertical row of diamonds. Even on the solid-color areas of an allover pattern, like the sock cuff, the carried yarn is twisted every 2 sts to maintain a consistent double-thick fabric. The sock instructions are given on p. 29.

(one strand). It needs to be twisted with the ground threads periodically so long floats are avoided. Sleeves were often knit with natural white and black yarns and dyed red after the knitting was completed.

Single motifs in different colors that look like intarsia are very complicated and rare. Some exceptional museum pieces have designs with as many as three contrasting colors. Nevertheless, true intarsia is unknown in *tvåändsstickning*. Most work is done in the round, and designs don't use large blocks of color. Isolated motifs, particularly on the back of a mitten or on the thumb gusset, are fairly common, though.

This type of motif is worked with two strands of the ground color and a separate contrasting thread for each pattern area. The pattern thread isn't carried around the knitting but is left hanging where it's used. On the next round, it's carried across the back of the motif to the point where it's needed. Since it shouldn't be carried more than 3 sts, if the block of contrasting color is larger, the knitter uses two contrasting threads—one jumping across the back from the middle to the beginning of the design, and the other from the end to the middle. This technique requires experience.

Embroidery

The fabric resulting from *tvåändsstickning* is firm and relatively inelastic, perfect for embroidering. Judging from the garments that have been preserved, embroidery was used mainly on mittens and gloves in Varmland and western Dalarna. These were worn for holidays and weddings and for church. Women's and men's gloves were embroidered with equal frequency.

Any embroidery technique that doesn't require the cutting of fabric can be used, and at some point probably was used. Many embellishments are free-form designs, similar to crewel embroidery; their bright colors and floral patterns could almost be mistaken for Hungarian embroideries (background of photo below). Others are more delicate and lacy, using straight stitches and outline or stem stitch. Not surprisingly, snowflake and star motifs are common. Counted-thread embroidery is also used, often with the reverse side of the knitting outward. Sollerösöm is a local form of counted-thread embroidery in which the stitches on the front are diagonal, and those on the reverse are horizontal. It's often intertwined with a second strand of yarn.

If you want to try embroidering your *tvåändsstickning*, mark the design outline with a washable marker or chalk. You could also just work free-hand, which is probably the way most of the historic examples were made. If you draw on the knitting, make sure your embroidery covers all the lines. Use tapestry wools or needlepoint yarn and a blunt tapestry needle.

For crewellike embroideries (inset photo below), use mostly satin stitch and outline or stem stitch for a more traditional look. Since you can't put the knitting in a hoop, you must pay special attention to the tension of your stitches. Don't pull them too tight. I've also found that if you pierce the knit stitches as you embroider, satin stitch will stay in place and cover better than if you go between stitches. However, go between knit stitches for counted-thread work. As with most embroidery, knots should be avoided. Ends should be woven through the embroidery on the reverse. They'll eventually felt, and they're less likely to come loose than if knots were used. ☐

Linda D. Y. Sokalski writes about single-color tvåändsstickning *in the article on p. 50.*

Linda D. Y. Sokalski writes about single-color tvåändsstickning *in the article on p. 50.*

Since the knit fabric is very firm, tvåändsstickning is ideal for elaborate free embroidery, as the detail of this mitten from Floda attests. (Photo courtesy of Dalarnas Museum). Sokalski's mittens (inset) use mostly satin and stem stitches.

Knitting Swedish socks

Modern Swedish knitters tend to prefer gray and white for *tvåändsstickning* socks. These socks should be made slightly large to allow for desired felting, which will make them even more durable and air-tight. You cast on at the ankle cuff, divide the stitches evenly on four needles, and knit around to the top of the heel. At this point, you place the lower-foot half of the stitches on a long thread and knit the upper-foot half of the stitches. When you get back around to the stitches on the thread, you pick up loops of the thread between the held stitches and treat these string loops as stitches to complete the round. You continue knitting this tubelike sock until you're at about the middle of the little toe. Then you decrease for the toe (step 7, pattern, facing page).

It's easier to work the heel last, but some knitters prefer to work it before completing the foot to aid in trying the sock on. When you remove the thread, you have a slashed opening between the cuff and the foot. You pick up the stitches that were placed on the thread for the top half of the heel. Then you pick up and work the loops that were knit from the thread for the bottom of the heel (photos, facing page). You decrease on each side of the top and bottom of the heel just as you worked the toe, grafting the last 8 sts together.

You can enlarge the sock's diameter by knitting it on a size larger needle for a slight increase or by casting on an extra 12 sts—a pattern multiple. There will be 3 more sts on each needle, and you'll need to begin and end the pattern for the top of the foot at a different place in the design.

This is an allover pattern with two colors. You use one strand of gray and one strand of white throughout. When knitting the solid-gray areas, twist in the white yarn every other stitch. Make your first twist after the first stitch on odd-numbered rounds and after the second stitch on even-numbered rounds. Give the strands a half-twist after each stitch on the lower-foot section; on the upper foot, twist the white yarn after every 2 sts in the gray-patterned areas of 3 sts or more.

The pattern for the socks in the photo on p. **27** was adapted from a photo in *Tvåändsstickat* (1984), by Birgitta Dandanell and Ulla Danielsson. The English translation of this book, *Twined Knitting* (1989), is available for $18.95 plus $2.50 S&H from Interweave Press, 306 N. Washington Ave., Loveland, CO 80537. —*L.D.Y.S.*

Swedish socks

This pattern is suitable for an experienced knitter. Directions are for size small to medium. Add stitches in multiples of 12 for larger sizes.

Materials: Sport-weight wool, gray—2½ oz. (☒ on chart), white—2 oz. (☐ on chart). Gotland yarn from Norsk Fjord Fiber, Rt. 2, Box 152, Lexington, GA 30648, would be ideal. Five double-pointed needles, size 3, or size needed to obtain gauge.

Gauge: 8 sts and 8 rows = 1 in.
To save time, take time to check gauge.

9. Heel pick-up: Remove thread holding 36 sts. Pick up 36 gray sts on 2 needles. Pick up all loops on opposite side of opening with 2 needles. Pick up 2 additional sts at each corner. Work across gray stitches, alternating gray and white yarns. Work first 2 corner sts. Work loops two at a time twice, alternating gray and white yarns: *Work first 2 loops together, drop only 1st loop. Work 2nd and 3rd loops together and drop 2nd loop.* * Repeat from * to * to complete loops. Work 2 corner sts.

8. Graft together stitches remaining on top and bottom of toe.

7. Decrease as shown: K2tog at end of needle 1 (gray) and needle 3 (white). Sl-k1-psso or SSK at beginning of needle 2 (white) and needle 4 (gray).

6. Knit in pattern to middle of little-toe length.

5. Rnd 31: Work needles 1-3. Run smooth thread through all stitches on needle 4, taking stitches off needle; and through last stitch on needle 3, keeping that stitch on needle. Pick up and work 18 string loops in pattern—1 loop between each held stitch. Then run same string through all stitches on needle 1; pick up and work 18 loops in pattern.

4. Twist white yarn in back every other stitch. Twist after odd-numbered stitches on odd rows, and even-numbered stitches on even rows. In pattern areas, twist after every 2 gray sts.

3. Divide stitches on row 2—18 sts per needle—to begin knitting in round.

2. Knit first row on reverse side, alternating gray and white.

1. Cast on 72 sts with double-twist method. Use gray in left hand; alternate gray and white in right hand.

Rnd 31 →

10. Heel: Work in alternating gray and white, shaping every round like toe decreases. Graft last 4 sts on top and bottom together.

11. Braid cast-on ends.

Needle 4   Needle 3   Needle 2   Needle 1

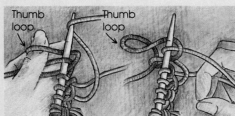

Thumb loop   Thumb loop

Double-twist cast-on: Insert needle from back of thumb loop. Alternate forming stitches with 2 right-hand strands. Bring thumb loop over each stitch to complete it.

The heel: After thread holder is removed, heel stitches are picked up around opening. Loops are worked two at a time.

Fair Isle Knitting

The versatile, traditional methods of stranded-color knitting in the round

by Alice Starmore

air Isle is situated northeast of mainland Scotland and slightly to the south of the Shetland Islands. This tiny island, which is barely three miles long and one mile wide, has given its name to what must now be the best known genre of British knitting.

Fair Isle knitting is a distinctive form of circular, stranded-color knitting (knitting with more than one color, in which the strand of yarn not in use is carried across the back of the work). The first samples appeared in the mid-19th century, when the Fair Islanders were producing gloves, stockings, caps, and tam-o'-shanters (berets named after a character in a Robert Burns poem). These items were decorated with bands of complex symmetrical patterns in unusual color combinations. The early patterns, now called traditional OXO patterns, consisted of six- or eight-sided lozenges, each containing a motif and linked horizontally by elaborate crosses.

History and development

Considering the complexity and sophistication of the pattern, color, and design of these early pieces, it is easy to understand the Victorians' curiosity regarding the origins of the technique. A popular legend grew that the Fair Isle pattern elements were of Spanish origin, due to the wrecking of the Armada ship El Gran Grifón on the shores of Fair Isle in 1588. This is a romantic idea, however; no samples or documentary records of Fair Isle patterns exist before the mid-19th century (although the hand-knitting industry of the Isles has been well documented since the 16th century).

Fair Islanders have always denied any Spanish connection with their craft. Their own story is that a Fair Isle sailor brought home a shawl decorated with patterns, which

the women copied and adapted in their knitting. More patterns were added as the style developed. The origin and fabric of the shawl remain a mystery, but the Shetland Islanders were great sea travelers and had close trading links with Scandinavia and the Baltic countries. Shetland was also a port of call for sailing ships outward bound for Iceland and America. A color explosion took place around 1800 in the knitting of the Scandinavian/Baltic area. Related styles of stranded-color knitting, influenced by the woven and embroidered textiles being exported throughout Europe, developed in Norway, Sweden, Finland, western Russia, Estonia, Latvia, and Lithuania. Many examples of 19th-century weaving, embroidery, and color knitting have survived, and while no examples are identical to those of Fair Isle, the same design elements and geometric symbols are found in the knitting of all of these countries. As a result of the differences in national character and cultural tradition, these common elements have been interpreted and applied in widely different ways.

The Fair Isle knitters were, and are, highly imaginative and inventive, and their work reveals a dislike of repetition. This trait became more apparent around 1900, when they began to work their patterns into fisher ganseys. (The word *gansey* is derived from Guernsey, one of the Channel Islands. A gansey is a pullover sweater, whose identifying characteristics are the gussets under the arms.) Many early examples were worked in bands of OXO patterns, each band containing a different motif from hem to shoulder. After 1910, the humble fisher gansey was adopted as an everyday garment for all classes, and Fair Isle knitting increased in popularity throughout mainland Britain. The technique was picked up by the mainland Shetland knitters, and the 1920s became a period of tremendous innovation, both in terms of pattern development and color.

Allover patterns appeared; some of them developed from the transposed OXO bands, and a few vertical allover patterns developed from OXO's that were set one above the other. Another major development was the introduction of hundreds of border patterns (9 to 13 rows) and peerie patterns

Fair Isle sweaters in traditional patterns. Top: A gansey with gussets. Each OXO band on the body contains a different motif. The pattern band on the top of the sleeve is the same as that on the body at the underarm. Knit by Jean Downton. Left: A sleeveless pullover in an allover diced pattern. The shaded colors here are based on the early colors of red, white, blue, and gold. Knit by Margaret Maciver. Center: A panel gansey with large stars flanked by vertical borders on back, front, and sleeves. The sides and underarms are filled with a seeding pattern. Knit by Catherine Matheson. Bottom: A child's cardigan in a vertical allover pattern, with slightly shaped armholes. Knit by Alice Starmore.

Fair Isle knitters often wear a leather belt while knitting in order to hold their work securely. The right needle is inserted into one of the holes in the pouch, which is stuffed with horsehair. The other needles hold the rest of the stitches in the round.

(1 to 7 rows). (Peerie is a Scottish word meaning *small*.) Many of these were taken directly from cross-stitch sampler booklets, which were available in great quantities. Large stars were added to the repertoire in the 1940s, coinciding with an influx of Norwegian refugees during World War II. In addition to becoming a favorite decoration on the backs of gloves and mittens, the stars were employed in vertical panels on ganseys, as in the center sweater in the photo on page 30. Moreover, with the availability of chemical dyes, which were brighter and faster than vegetable dyes, came a color explosion. Continuous experimentation has led to the mastery of color combination, for which Shetland knitters are now justly famous.

Today, the Shetland knitters have a vast repertoire of patterns and a wide array of colors available with which to create endless, unique designs. For an imaginative knitter this is indeed a happy position. Sadly, though, in the Shetlands and in Fair Isle, knitting as a cottage industry is on the decline. Copies of the traditional sweaters are produced by machine, and many knitters find more financially rewarding work in the oil-related industries of which the Shetland Islands have become a center. The craft itself, however, is very much alive, and knitters produce garments for their families as well as fill orders for shops in the Shetlands and abroad.

Techniques

Fair Isle circular knitting is generally worked with four straight 14-in. needles. This needle length is even used for small-scale work, but most knitters will find it easier if the length is appropriate to the garment size. For a wide garment, it is advisable to use

five needles in order to cope comfortably with all the stitches.

Cast the total number of stitches onto one needle; then divide them as evenly as possible over three needles. Making sure the cast-on edge isn't twisted, join the three needles into the shape of a triangle, and begin the round by working the fourth needle into the first cast-on stitch (see drawing on page 33). Then proceed around the triangle, marking the first stitch to indicate the beginning of each new round.

This method has several advantages over flat knitting, especially for patterned work: The right side always faces the knitter, which means the pattern is visible as it is being worked, making for easier and faster progress; the resulting fabric is of a more even tension, as the knitter works continuously in knit stitch; and the need for seams is eliminated, which produces a neater finish and again allows for faster working.

Fair Isle knitters favor the circular technique to such an extent that they bridge openings, such as armholes and cardigan fronts, by working "steeks" (in Scottish, *steek* means *to fasten,* or *to close*), thus allowing the work to continue in the round. (See "Gansey knitting," page 33.) Steeks are wide ladders of yarn that are formed when an opening is knit. The steek is later cut open so that the sleeve or border stitches can be knit up (see drawing, page 33).

Stranded-color knitting—To work the colored patterns of Fair Isle knitting, you must work two colors in the same round—the background color and a pattern color. The yarn not in use is carried along the back of the work.

Hold the yarn in use with the right hand (if you are right-handed) and the yarn not

The seaside meadows, moorlands, and skies of the Isle of Lewis inspire Starmore's use of color in her Fair Isle gansey sweater patterns.

in use with the left hand. Knit the required number of stitches in the first color. Then carry the second color loosely across the back of the work, and knit the required number of stitches in this color. Do not pull the stranded yarn tightly across the back, as this will cause the knitting to bunch up. At the same time, do not make gigantic loops, as this, too, will produce uneven tension, and the large loops will catch and possibly break. The ideal is to achieve an even tension with loops that lie flat on the back of the work.

All traditional Fair Isle garments have an unusual colored rib pattern known as corrugated rib, which is also worked with two colors in one round. This pattern is used wherever a firm edge is required, as in welts, cuffs, and necks. Corrugated rib is a k2, p2 rib that uses one color for the knit stitches and a contrasting color for the purl stitches. Be sure to move the yarn to the back of the rib after working the p2 so that all strands are carried across the back of the work.

Pattern and color—Most Fair Isle patterns are small and symmetrical, with four or eight similar motifs. The pattern usually has an odd number of rows so that there is a center row, often accentuated with color. The patterns also do not have large areas of one color, the aim being to keep both colors moving as much as possible.

There are literally hundreds of Fair Isle patterns, and only a small selection is shown here. Nevertheless, with an imaginative use of pattern and color combinations, the knitter can achieve many varied results. Fair Isle patterns can be classified into seven

categories, as shown in the drawing on pages 34 and 35: traditional OXO patterns, 15 and 17 rows; peerie patterns, 1 to 7 rows (mainly used between border patterns); border patterns, 9 to 13 rows; allover patterns; seeding patterns; large stars; peaked and waved patterns (the "peaks" and "waves" are shaded from light to dark).

Seeding patterns are used to fill spaces between large patterns and therefore keep the colors moving. The panel gansey (center sweater in photo) on page 30 illustrates a typical use of seeding. The panel of large stars is worked up the center of the back, the front, and the sleeves, with a border pattern worked vertically at each side of the large stars. The rest of the patterned area is worked in seeding.

Joining devices are used to link motifs and keep the colors moving between them, thus creating a good, workable pattern. The 15-row traditional OXO pattern (top sweater in photo on page 30, and top of drawing, page 34) isolates a motif (O) and a cross (X) put together to form a pattern. Pattern repeats, in other words, the number of stitches it takes to work the pattern once horizontally, can be varied, depending on the width of the joining device. This means the knitter can choose a pattern repeat that will fit an exact number of times into the total number of stitches in the garment body.

There are two basic rules that apply to all Fair Isle knitting patterns. The first is absolute, and the second is more of a guiding principle:
Rule 1: Only two colors are to be used in any one row or round.
Rule 2: The degree of contrast between the background color and pattern color should

remain as constant as possible throughout all color changes. This will ensure that the pattern is distinct throughout.

Color schemes can be as simple or complex as the knitter chooses. Some Fair Isle working ganseys have only two colors, but the majority have several, with background and pattern colors changing frequently. Color changing follows the symmetry of the patterns, and often the center row is picked out for special treatment, as in the bottom drawing on the facing page.

Despite what I have said, it is important for the knitter to realize that color choice is still a matter of individual taste. Just as the Fair Isle knitters discovered, I have found that experimentation and practice are the best ways to achieve success. It is perhaps wise for the beginner to start out with a scheme for a few well-balanced colors before attempting anything that is too complex. As with simple patterns, a simple, well-thought-out color scheme can be very striking.

Pleasing color schemes surround us all in many forms, both natural and man-made, and we should be inspired and influenced by them. Paintings, Persian carpets, weaving, gardens, flowers, landscapes—anything that takes our fancy is fair game for interpretation in Fair Isle. I live on the wild and windswept Isle of Lewis in the Outer Hebrides and am constantly inspired by its seaside, moorland, skies, and landscapes.

Alice Starmore is a knitwear designer in Scotland. The garments and samples shown were knit in two-ply jumper-weight yarn supplied by Messrs. Jamieson & Smith (SWB) Ltd. Photos on pages 31, 32 and 34 by author.

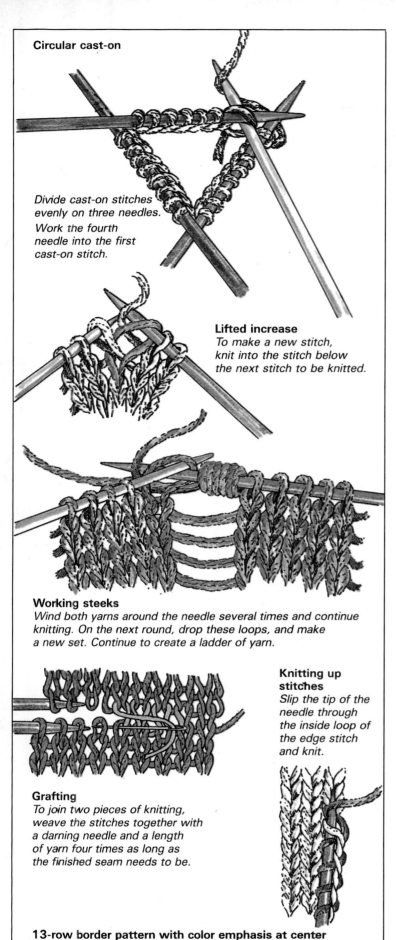

Circular cast-on

Divide cast-on stitches evenly on three needles. Work the fourth needle into the first cast-on stitch.

Lifted increase
To make a new stitch, knit into the stitch below the next stitch to be knitted.

Working steeks
Wind both yarns around the needle several times and continue knitting. On the next round, drop these loops, and make a new set. Continue to create a ladder of yarn.

Grafting
To join two pieces of knitting, weave the stitches together with a darning needle and a length of yarn four times as long as the finished seam needs to be.

Knitting up stitches
Slip the tip of the needle through the inside loop of the edge stitch and knit.

13-row border pattern with color emphasis at center

Gansey Knitting

A number of specific techniques are employed in gansey knitting. The points at which you need to use these techniques in knitting a gansey sweater are indicated in the drawing on page 37.

Techniques
Lifted increase—This is sometimes referred to as an invisible increase and is used throughout the gansey. To make a new stitch, knit into the stitch below the next stitch to be knit.

Steeks—This is the method of bridging an opening (such as a cardigan front) so that knitting may proceed in the round.

Both yarns are wound loosely around the needle several times at the appropriate place in the round. In the next round, these loops are dropped off the needle, and a new set is made. A wide ladder of yarns is formed. Upon completion of the opening, the steek is cut open. (The yarn ends are darned in on the wrong side.) An extra stitch is worked at each side of the steek so that, after the steek is cut open, the stitches for sleeve or border—whichever the case may be—can be knitted up through the extra stitches.

At openings too wide to bridge with steeks (e.g., at necklines), the knitter divides the garment by separating the stitches for back and front. The neck-front stitches are placed on a holder. The right and left neck/shoulder and back are worked separately, flat, on two needles. The garment is worked as in flat knitting, but the knitter works on the right side, breaking off yarns at the end of each row. All ends are darned in when the garment is complete.

Knitting up stitches—Slip the tip of the needle through the inside loop of the edge stitch and knit. Stitches are knitted up so there are no seams. For example, sleeve stitches are knitted up around the armhole, and the sleeve is knitted down to the bottom instead of being knit separately and then sewn. Front bands of cardigans and armhole bands of slipovers are also knitted up. This technique is neater and produces a much better finish than bulky seams.

Grafting—Grafting joins two pieces of knitting. A row of stitches between the two pieces of knitting is made with a darning needle, thus forming another row and making an invisible seam.

Hold the two pieces of knitting so the stitches butt up against each other. Thread a darning needle with a length of yarn the same color as the knitting and about four times the seam length. The stitches are slipped off the needles a few at a time as you weave the stitches together, as shown in the drawing at left.

Knitting guidelines
1. Mark the first stitch to indicate the beginning of each round.
2. After working the increase round, mark the first and center stitches. These are the seam stitches. They are positioned at the center underarms, thus dividing the body into back and front.
3. The gusset is begun while the body is being knit. To work the gusset, inc 1 st at each side of the seam stitch; then work 3 rounds straight; continue in this way, increasing 1 st at each side of the gusset on every 4th round until you reach the armhole. Then place the gusset stitches on a holder, and knit the rest of the body. Pick up the gusset stitches with the sleeve stitches, and decrease the gusset at each side of every 4th round until only the seam stitch remains. Then begin the sleeve decreasing.
4. Knit up the armhole stitches by knitting into every stitch. Sometimes knitting into every stitch will result in too many stitches, and the sleeve will flare out at the shoulder. The more even the tension, the better the result. It is preferable to work this out while you're knitting rather than to calculate it beforehand. The most accurate method, while a bit tedious, is to knit into every stitch and judge with your eye as you progress and then to knit 3 or 4 rounds. If the knitting looks as if it is flaring out, rip it out and knit up fewer stitches. Beware of knitting up too few stitches, however, as this will look equally awful. The important thing is to knit up the stitches evenly so the sleeve emerges straight from the shoulder.
5. Work sleeve decreases in pairs, one k2tog, and one k2tog through back loops, at each side of the seam stitch.
6. Fair Isle knitters often use a knitting belt to keep their knitting rigid and secure. The belt is made of leather and fastened with a buckle. The right needle is inserted into the holed pouch, which is stuffed with a material such as horsehair, which is loose enough so the needle can be inserted, yet firm enough to hold the needle in place. Knitting belts and authentic Shetland yarns are available from Messrs. Jamieson & Smith (SWB) Ltd., 90 North Rd., Lerwick, Shetland Isles ZE1 OPQ, United Kingdom.

Fair Isle patterns

One square in a chart represents one stitch in a row or round. The black square represents the pattern color, and the empty square represents the background color. Begin working from the chart at the bottom row, and read from right to left across one horizontal repeat of the pattern. (The drawings on this page and page 36 illustrate how to isolate and vary a pattern repeat. Always mark out the repeat at the center of the pattern.)

Most traditional OXO motifs (15-row and 17-row) and joining devices may be combined for any pattern repeat and for varied effect, but place them so both colors are moving at reasonable intervals.

Border and peerie combinations offer infinite possibilities, and many Fair Isle knitters use a different border pattern of the same size throughout a garment (e.g., 9/3/9/3 rows repeated throughout, using a different 9-row pattern each time). A number of different-sized peeries and borders can work together (3/9/3/1/11/1 repeated throughout, for example), but a simple, well-thought-out scheme can be effective too. A few plain rows between patterns create an interesting effect.

Shown here are bands of traditional OXO patterns in the traditional colors of natural white, red (from madder), gold (from a local vegetable dye), blue (from indigo), and natural dark brown. Each band contains different variations on the motifs.

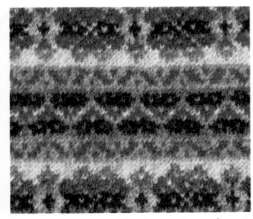

An arrangement of border and peerie patterns. Border patterns are 9-row to 13-row patterns; peerie patterns are 1-row to 7-row patterns, as shown in the drawings on the facing page. Hundreds of these patterns developed as Fair Isle knitting became popular throughout mainland Britain in the 1920s.

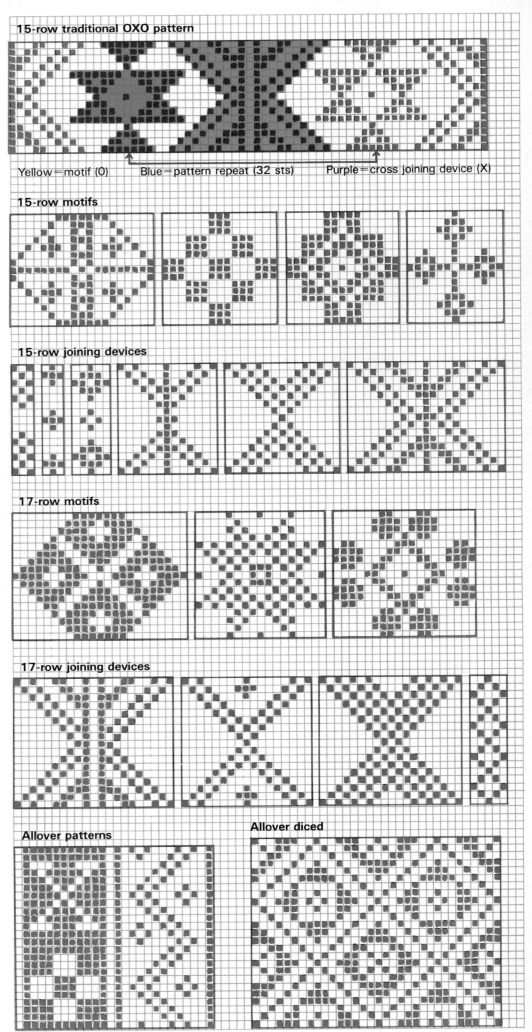

15-row traditional OXO pattern

Yellow = motif (O)   Blue = pattern repeat (32 sts)   Purple = cross joining device (X)

15-row motifs

15-row joining devices

17-row motifs

17-row joining devices

Allover patterns

Allover diced

2-row peeries

3-row peeries

4-row peeries

5-row peeries

6-row peeries

7-row peeries

Seeding patterns

9-row borders

11-row borders

13-row borders

19-row star

Peaked pattern

Wave pattern

25-row star

Designing a Fair Isle gansey

The traditional Fair Isle gansey is a basic sweater shape with a round neck and dropped shoulder line. Similar to all British fisher ganseys, the Fair Isle features a diamond-shaped gusset underarm. The gusset makes movement easier (fishermen use their arms constantly, hauling nets, etc.) and reduces the strain on a weak part of the garment. Many modern ganseys omit the gusset, and some have shaped armholes. However, besides being traditional, the gusset is attractive and practical and well worth including in a design.

These instructions are a detailed blueprint for designing and working out the calculations needed to knit a gansey. Not all Fair Isle patterns are so precise. Some don't repeat exactly into the horizontal and vertical measurements, and unfinished horizontal repeats are hidden at the seam stitch where the round begins. This is acceptable, but I feel that the symmetry of pattern and color should be emphasized by their symmetrical placement. Vertical repeats are more easily dealt with. If the pattern doesn't match at the shoulders, it can be finished at a complete repeat, and the remaining length worked in a seeding pattern to make an attractive seeded panel on the shoulder.

I'd like to encourage you to work on your own and not follow exact instructions. For the purposes of illustration, however, in the diagram I have provided the measurements for a classic gansey to fit a 36-in. to 38-in. bust/chest. This example will make it easier for you to understand the relationship of the measurements in the calculations given in parentheses throughout the text. You can use these measurements as exact instructions, provided your tension is exactly 8 sts and 8½ rows to 1 in. The yarn I use to achieve this tension is Jamieson & Smith's two-ply jumper-weight Shetland, which is a classic Fair Isle knitting weight.

Measurements—Draw a diagram of the gansey, and note on it the exact measurements you need for the following:
(A) Chest: At least 2 in. more than the actual body measurement.
(B) Length from top of shoulder to base of sweater.
(C) Length from underarm to base of sweater.
(D) Armhole width.
(E) Back-neck width.
(F) Neck drop: 2 in. for a child; 2½ in. for a small adult; 3 in. for a large adult.
(G) Sleeve length.
(H) Sleeve width at top of cuff.

Tension—To establish the number of stitches and rows required for these measurements, you must knit a patterned tension-gauge swatch, using the correct yarn and needles. You can also experiment with colors and patterns while working the tension-gauge swatch. It can be a circular piece of about a hand's width or a flat piece worked on two double-pointed needles, with yarns broken off at the end of each row and restarted, or joined in, on the right side of every new row. Cast on enough stitches so the piece measures at least 4 in. by 4 in. when laid flat.

To calculate your tension, lay the piece on a flat surface and pin it down at the edges, being careful not to stretch it. Using a firm ruler, note the exact number of stitches and rows to 1 in. Remember to count half stitches and half rows—a half stitch in 1 in. means 20 sts in a 40-in. width!

Horizontal pattern repeats—Calculate the number of stitches required for the body by multiplying the chest measurement (A) by the stitch tension. (For example, 40-in. chest x 8 sts to the inch=320 sts for the sweater body.)

Divide your body stitches by the number of pattern repeats. Ideally, the patterns should repeat an even number of times around the body so the gansey will be perfectly symmetrical. (For example, a 32-stitch pattern will fit 10 times into a 320-stitch body, with 5 full patterns on the front and back.)

The exception to this rule is a vertical allover pattern, where the pattern is asymmetrical. In this case, the opposite rule applies, and the pattern should be repeated an odd number of times so it corresponds on the garment front and back. Draw up the finalized pattern on graph paper.

Corrugated rib—The corrugated rib requires fewer stitches and smaller size needles than the sweater body so that the rib is not too wide. Divide the number of body stitches by approximately 8 if you want an average rib, or by approximately 10 if you want it a little tighter. Reduce the number of body stitches by that amount to determine the number of stitches you need to cast on for the sweater rib. Make sure the resulting number will be evenly divisible by 4. Corrugated rib is a 4-stitch repeat (k2, p2), and in order to ensure that the rib is correct all around the garment, the number of stitches must be divisible by 4. If it is not, add or subtract to adjust it. As the adjustment will be 3 sts at the most, it will not make a great deal of difference to the overall width. (320 sts for body÷8=40. 320−40=280 sts to cast on for the rib.)

Vertical pattern repeats—Calculate and note the length of the patterned area by subtracting the rib length from measurement B (the length from top of shoulder to base of sweater). Calculate the number of rounds required for the length by multiplying the tension gauge by the length of the patterned area. (If measurement B−rib length=22 in., and the row tension is 8½ rows to 1 in., 187 rounds are required for the patterned length of the body: 22x8½=187.)

Then calculate the number of pattern repeats that will divide evenly into this number. If necessary, reduce or increase the rib length so the patterns match at the shoulder, either at the center of a pattern or at a completed pattern. Calculate and note the number of patterned rounds required to the underarm in the same way: measurement C−rib length.

The gusset—To plan the size and starting point of the gusset, use the stitch gauge to determine the number of stitches required at its widest point (approximately 2½ in. for a small size and 3 in. for a large). The number of stitches needed will always be an odd number, as the gusset begins by increasing at each side of a central stitch.

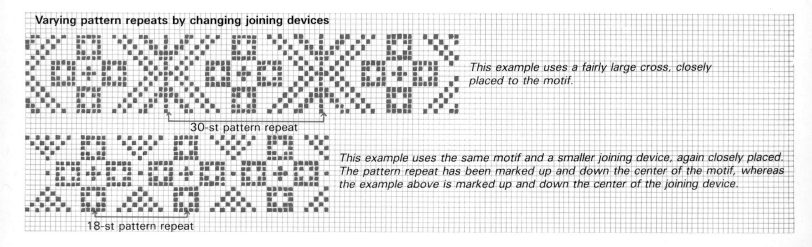

Varying pattern repeats by changing joining devices

30-st pattern repeat

This example uses a fairly large cross, closely placed to the motif.

18-st pattern repeat

This example uses the same motif and a smaller joining device, again closely placed. The pattern repeat has been marked up and down the center of the motif, whereas the example above is marked up and down the center of the joining device.

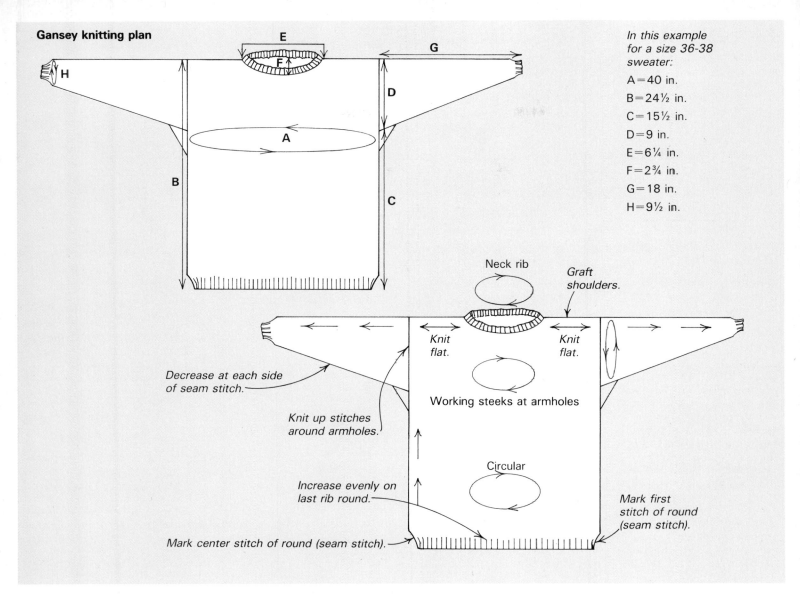

Gansey knitting plan

E

F

H

A

B

C

D

G

In this example for a size 36-38 sweater:

A = 40 in.
B = 24½ in.
C = 15½ in.
D = 9 in.
E = 6¼ in.
F = 2¾ in.
G = 18 in.
H = 9½ in.

Neck rib

Graft shoulders.

Knit flat.

Knit flat.

Working steeks at armholes

Decrease at each side of seam stitch.

Knit up stitches around armholes.

Circular

Increase evenly on last rib round.

Mark first stitch of round (seam stitch).

Mark center stitch of round (seam stitch).

To calculate the number of rounds required from the first increase to the last (increasing every 4th round), use this formula: Rounds required=(Total number of increased stitches x 2)−3. (For example: Number of stitches in gusset=21, so number of stitches increased=20. Rounds required: [20x2]−3=37. The gusset begins 37 rounds before the underarm, which is measurement C−rib length.)

Neck—Calculate and note how many rounds in the neck drop (measurement F), and note where the front-neck shaping begins, based on your design. Calculate how many stitches are in the back neck (measurement E).

Shape the front neck by placing roughly two thirds of the number of stitches in E on a holder at the center front neck, and reduce the remainder on each side within the F number of rounds. (For example: If F=20 rows and E=49 sts, approximately ⅔

of E for front neck=31 sts. Remaining stitches to be reduced=49−31=18. Therefore, reduce 9 sts at each side, evenly within 20 rows [every 2nd row plus 2 rows straight].) At this stage *check all calculations* and knit the body of the gansey. Before starting to knit, read "Knitting guidelines" on page 33.

The sleeve—Knit up the stitches *evenly* around the armhole by knitting into the extra stitch at the edge (see drawing, page 33). Note the number of stitches knit up and work out the sleeve as follows:

Calculate the number of pattern rounds required for the sleeve length (measurement G−rib length), and, if necessary, adjust the rib so that you'll end with a complete pattern. Remember to begin the sleeve pattern at the body underarm, and work downward so the pattern will match across the body and sleeve when the sweater is worn. (Note the sleeve

pattern on the traditional sweater on page 30.)

Calculate the number of stitches required for the sleeve at the top of the cuff (measurement H). In order to calculate the number of stitches to be decreased down the sleeve, add 1 st (seam stitch) to the number knit up around the armhole, and subtract measurement H. (142 armhole sts+1 seam stitch=143 sts. Measurement H=77 sts. Number of stitches to be decreased: 143−77=66.)

To place the decreases evenly down the sleeve, subtract the gusset rounds from the total patterned sleeve rounds, and divide the result (the remaining patterned sleeve rounds) by half the stitches to be decreased (2 sts are decreased in 1 round). This will tell you how frequently you need to decrease along the sleeve length. (Total patterned rounds [measurement G−rib length]=136. Gusset rounds=37.

Remaining sleeve rounds: 136−37=99. Half the number of decreases=33. 99÷33=3. Therefore, decrease 2 sts every 3rd round.)

You should also work a decrease round around the bottom of the sleeve before beginning the cuff rib so the rib will be tighter than the sleeve. Make sure the resulting number is divisible by 4.

Center the sleeve pattern—To center the pattern on the sleeve, divide the number of stitches knitted up around the armhole by the number of stitches in one pattern repeat. (Stitches knit up around armhole=142. Stitches in one pattern repeat=19. Repeats across sleeve: 142÷19=7 repeats+11 sts.)

To center the pattern on the sleeve, work the last 5 sts of the pattern repeat, repeat the 19 pattern sts 7 times, and then work the first 6 sts of the pattern repeat. □

Argyles *without* Seams

A new technique lets you knit an entire garment diamond by diamond

by Suzann Thompson

*a*rgyles—sweaters and socks with crosshatched, interlocking diamonds—have been popular for decades, but they have always been difficult to knit because you must use intarsia. That is: each diamond in a row requires its own bobbin or ball of yarn, and you have to twist the yarns between each color change. You always have seams because you can't work intarsia in the round.

But store-bought argyle socks are seamless. I contemplated my socks for a long time before my practical husband suggested I unravel one to find out how this paradox is accomplished. If you have a commercial argyle sock you can part with, cut off its foot. Start unraveling the leg. You can pull out an entire diamond before anything happens to the next one. In contrast, when you unravel a hand-knit argyle, you must take out one row of each diamond across every row.

In a machine-knitted argyle, each diamond is knitted separately back and forth, and the machine completes all the diamonds of one color in the course before proceeding to diamonds in another color. As it knits each diamond in the second color course, the machine joins them row by row to the previous set of diamonds using a machine version of short rowing.

Once I understood the machine technique, I could begin to translate it to handknitting. The toughest problem was how to link the courses of diamonds. I tried several methods, but I kept getting gaps or twists. Finally, I hit upon the method I'll be describing here. The key is to pick up in the thread that runs between the second and third stitches from the edge of a completed diamond when you're increasing the sides of a new diamond. This joins the diamonds securely and nearly invisibly, much like wrapping does for short rows in handknitting (see *Threads* No. 39, p. 18).

Seamless argyle knitting relieves most of the frustrations of the traditional method. You only knit with one color at a time (two if you're crosshatching, but these one-stitch lines are easy to handle). And since you knit one complete diamond at a time, you can knit right from the ball (no bobbins). You never have to worry about twists or color changes, and because you can complete a single diamond pretty quickly, the work seems to

All the experts will tell you that this vest couldn't have been knitted without seams. Author Suzann Thompson did the impossible and figured out how to knit argyles one diamond at a time with short rows. (Photo by Susan Kahn)

Sampler 1: Shaping the sides of a diamond (explanation at right)

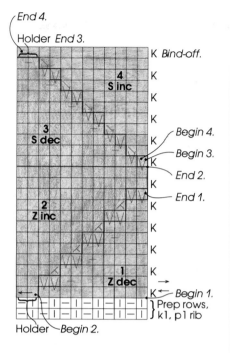

Key

⋁	Slip st pwise (wyib for knitting, wyif for purling)
⊞	Pick up thread between two sts from underneath
⧄	K2tog, picked-up thread and slipped st
⊞⋁	On p side (read left to right): pick up thread between sts 2 and 3; slip st 1; p2tog, picked-up thread and slipped st
I / —	Knit / Purl — Rib shown as appears from right side

To start filling in a diamond, you put the held stitches from the two diamonds below onto double-pointed needles and slip the two base stitches onto the left-hand needle. All the other stitches remain on holders.

1. Z decrease—upper left side

Prep: Cast on 12 sts. Work 2 rows k1, p1 rib.

Begin Z dec and set up base for fill-in diamond:

1. K10, place last 2 sts on holder, turn.
2. Z dec (WS rows): Sl 1 (blue symbol), p to end.
3. Z dec (RS rows): K 2 fewer sts than previous k row, turn. (Sl st and first p st from previous row remain on LHN.)
4. End WS: Sl 1, p1, break yarn.

Notes: Each row you k or p1 st less than on previous row. Sts on needle separate into pairs with gap before each sl st.

2. Z increase—lower right side

Begin Z inc: With new color, k 2 sts on holder, turn.

1. Use third needle to p 2 sts; *p1 st from first triangle (a sl st), sl 1 (pink symbol), then insert tip of RHN under thread between next 2 sts on LHN (a pair); turn. *
2. Z inc (RS rows): K2tog (picked-up thread and sl st), k to end.
3. Z inc (WS rows): P new color sts, rep *-*, (step 1).
4. Last WS row: P to last st, sl last st, turn.
5. K all sts, turn; p all sts, turn.

Notes: On each p row, p 2 sts more than on previous p row. Pick-up thread is between next complete pair. On each knit row, k2tog, then k same number of sts as previous p row. (See photos on p. 40.)

3. S decrease—upper right side

Begin S dec: Use same color to complete top half of half-diamond.

1. S dec (RS rows): Sl 1 (pink symbols), k to end.
2. S dec (WS rows): P 2 sts fewer than previous p row (leave sl st and first k st from previous row on LHN), turn.
3. Last RS row: Sl 1, k3. Last WS row: P2, place 2 p sts on holder, break yarn.

Note: Sts separate into pairs, as Z dec.

4. S increase—lower left side

Begin S inc: Use new color.

1. With RS facing, k1 from low end of needle (first sl st in S dec), turn.
2. S inc (WS rows): With yarn in front, insert tip of LHN under thread between 2nd and 3rd sts on RHN (a pair); swing LHN leftward to slip first st of RHN to LHN (blue symbols); insert RHN into slipped st and picked-up thread and p2tog (see photos on p. 41); p sts on LHN; turn.
3. S inc (RS rows): K 2 sts more than on previous k row, turn.
4. Last WS row: Pick up thread between sts on holder, and work as usual. Last RS row: To complete sampler, bind off all sts, including 2 on holder.

To fill in the right-hand side of a diamond, you use **Z increases**, which begin on the purl side: Having purled all the stitches already in the new diamond's color, you purl the first stitch of the adjacent diamond, slip the next to your RHN, and then pick up the thread between the second and third stitches, at left. Then turn the work and knit the slipped stitch and the picked-up thread together.

Sampler 2: Argyling—full diamonds

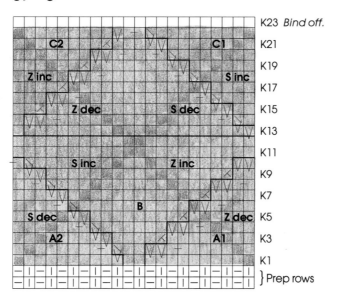

K23 *Bind off.*
K21   C2   C1
K19
K17   Z inc   S inc
K15   Z dec   S dec
K13
K11
K9   S inc   Z inc
K7
K5   S dec   B   Z dec
K3   A2   A1
K1
} *Prep rows*

Prep: *Cast on 22 sts. Work 2 rows k1, p1 rib. (Omit crosshatch first time.)*

1. *Put A2 sts on holder. Put B sts on another holder.*

2. *Work **A1** following Z-dec directions from sampler 1: Begin k10, turn; sl 1, p9; etc. Break yarn. Place A1 sts on holder.*

3. *Place **A2** sts on needle. K all sts first row, then follow S-dec directions. Last row: p1, turn, sl st to RHN.*

4. Begin B: *With RS facing, slip two B sts from holder to LHN (A2 sts are already on it). Place A1 sts on RHN.*

5. *With new color, k2 (B sts), turn.*
WS: S inc, purl B sts, Z inc, turn.
RS: Finish Z inc, knit B sts, k1, turn.
***Note:** For last S inc, because of sampler being flat, pick up thread from edge as best you can. On same row, sl last st for Z inc, turn. K all sts, turn, p 1 row.*

6. Begin decreasing B diamond:
S dec: sl first st, k to 1 st from end, turn.
Z dec: sl first st, p to 2 sts from end, turn.
Work 2 fewer sts per row. Last row: sl 1, p2.

7. *Place p2 sts on holder; place st on left edge, low end, on holder.*

8. *Work **C1:** S inc. For last WS row, pick up thread between two B sts on holder.*
***Note:** For garment with full diamonds, you would next dec C1.*

9. *Work **C2:** Z inc. Start on RS: k1 (left edge st on holder); turn, and work first Z inc. Last WS row: P all sts up to two B sts.*
***Note:** For garment you would now dec C2 diamond.*

10. To finish swatch: *Purl across B and C1 sts. Then bind off all sts on next k row.*
***Note:** You must work an extra p row on C1 sts to do this.*

grow much faster. You do, however, have about the same number of ends to finish since you must break the yarn at the end of each diamond.

Practicing the technique

I've designed two samplers to help you master this technique. You need double-pointed needles and a large supply of stitch holders (see the photo on p. 39). Sampler 1 (p. 39), which is only half a diamond wide, teaches you how to make each of the diamond's sides, one at a time. Sampler 2 at left introduces you to full diamonds—true argyling—on which you must work both increasing sides or both decreasing sides on each row. Once you understand the principle, you can make any size seamless argyle garment. To work both swatches, you'll need an ounce each of two or three colors, three double-pointed needles, and two small stitch holders.

Sampler 1—Looking at the chart for the first sampler on p. 39, you'll see that you first decrease stitches in the lower green area to make the green triangle. Next you fill in (increase) the adjacent purple triangle and then decrease it (almost the same way you decreased the green one). Finally, you fill in the upper green triangle. I refer to the increases and decreases as "S" or "Z," depending on whether they lean to the left (S) or to the right (Z), like the center strokes of those letters.

As you knit, you'll notice that when you work the decrease angles by slipping a stitch on one row and working to one stitch before the slipped stitch on the next row, the slipped stitch and the unworked stitch group on the needle into a pair. The increases are produced between the paired stitches. You can see how I make Z increases at upper left, and S increases are shown on the facing page.

Sampler 2—Since my method has you work each diamond separately, completing one color course before filling in the next, I label all the diamonds (or partial diamonds) in one course by the same letter and consecutive numbers. The half diamonds of A are first, B is the first course to consist of full diamonds, next is C, and so on. I knit all the A's first, in numerical order, then the B's, and right on through the alphabet.

Try knitting Sampler 2 (directions at left) without crosshatching the first time to accustom yourself to working Z and S decreases and Z and S increases at each side of a diamond. This way you'll only have to master one new skill at a time.

You'll notice three slight changes from Sampler 1: Because this sampler is flat, you will have to reach all the way to the edge to find a thread to pick up for the last S inc on the B diamond (row 10). You won't have this problem in a circular garment. Also, on row 1 of the S dec on A2, you don't slip the first stitch because it's already on a holder to be worked in the B diamond. Similarly, on the last row of the Z inc on C2 (row 22), you merely purl all the stitches up to the holder containing the two B stitches. These changes will allow the pairs to form as they should. Also note that the odd courses, A and C, will be two stitches narrower than the even course(s), B, true for all garments.

Working the crosshatch—Knit the practice piece again, this time adding in the crosshatch color. Remember to twist yarns at the color change (see *Basics, Threads* No. 41, p. 16). When using this extra color, pay close attention to it as it approaches the edges of a diamond. It may be required for the decrease stitch on Z or S increase angles (row 6—S inc). On row 17, when you're filling the C diamonds, be careful not to knit the crosshatch color prematurely.

If your crosshatching is just one color, try this hint I learned from Anne Macdonald, the guru of traditional argyle knitting: Cut a piece of yarn long enough to work two entire crosshatches. Find the middle point of this yarn. Knit the begin-

ning of the crosshatch (the two stitches in the center of a diamond) with the middle point of the crosshatch yarn. Use one end of the yarn to work the crosshatch in one direction, and the other end for the other direction. To avoid having so many ends to sew in, wind the ends into yarn butterflies (see *Threads* No. 41, p. 16), and unwind them as the crosshatches grow.

Working in the round

You can knit a seamless argyle sweater or sock by adapting a seamed pattern. Find a pattern where the diamonds increase and decrease one stitch each side every row, as in the samplers. (Patternworks has a booklet of sock patterns that includes argyles—PO Box 1690, Poughkeepsie, NY 12601; 914-462-8000). Also, choose diamonds that are an even number of stitches wide so the decrease pairs will work out correctly. It's also easiest to work with a pattern where diamonds always meet with two stitches touching. If the pattern includes an extra stitch or two for the seam; mark out those stitches. Some argyle sock patterns also have a split heel. Either rewrite the pattern, combining the heel halves, or find a circular sock pattern with a similar heel.

To help you visualize the sock (or sweater) in the round, make a photocopy of the graph, outline the diamonds, mark the rows "k" or "p," and label the diamonds

A1, A2, B1, B2, and so on (as shown on the schematic drawing of my vest, below). Then cut the photocopy out, and tape it together along the seamline. You'll notice that the single B stitches at each edge meet to form a pair of B stitches for the diamond that replaces the seam. Number the rows, make notes regarding shaping, and as you knit, scribble lots of notes to help you remember where you are.

The corners where diamonds meet can be loose and messy looking. Use the yarn ends to tidy up by tightening beginning and ending stitches that are too loose before you sew in and trim the ends.

You can also customize your socks by tapering them, but I suggest that you become thoroughly familiar with argyling in the round first. For sock shaping, see the information on p. 63 and 66; and Betty Amos' discussion of shaping knee socks in *Homespun Handknit* (ed. L. Ligon, Interweave Press, 1987; pp. 149-150). When you begin the instep and gusset shaping after you've turned the heel, you need to complete the diamonds on the instep while at the same time shaping the gusset. You'll keep working back and forth until all the diamonds have been completed. Then you can finish the sock with circular knitting. □

Suzann Thompson is a free-lance knitting designer. She lives in Austin, TX.

*An **S increase** fills in the left-hand side of a diamond and is completed on the purl side. After working one stitch of the previous colored diamond on the knit side, you turn the work. Pick up the thread between the second and third stitches on the right-hand needle (left).*

Then you swing the left-hand needle back toward the left to slip the first stitch from the right-hand needle onto it (right).

Finally, you purl the thread and stitch together (left).

Circular argyle vest schematic (small)
(Measurements in inches)

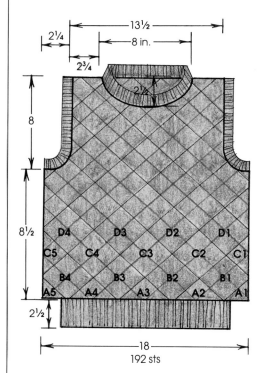

13½
2¼
8 in.
2¾
2¼
8
8½
2½
18
192 sts
D4 D3 D2 D1
C5 C4 C3 C2 C1
B4 B3 B2 B1
A5 A4 A3 A2 A1

Diamonds in odd courses (A, C, etc.) are 22 sts wide. Last row differs from Sampler 2 (step 6): sl 1, p2, turn, sl 1.

Diamonds in even courses (B, D, etc.) are 24 sts wide. To join corners to each other, complete every other diamond. On full k row of fill-ins, sl last st, pick up thread behind two sts on next B diamond, k2tog—sl st and thread. Join other corner at end of p row similarly.

To start C: sl 1 from RHN to LHN; k2, turn, S inc, p2, Z inc.

Methods for Multicolored Knitting

How to manage many strands

by Maggie Righetti

One of the joys of hand knitting is making traditional multicolored patterns, and some of the loveliest are the Nordic and Fair Isle designs. Wonderful patterns, like snowflakes, hearts and flowers, fleurs-de-lis, and crests and crosses, emerge as the colors interplay along stockinette rows.

The traditional method is to knit these patterns in the round on straight, double-pointed needles. More recently, they have been knit on circular needles. All the colors that are needed for a given round are carried along behind the work as the knitting progresses, leaving floats of the unused yarns on the wrong side of the fabric. The completed tube is simply cut for cardigan-sweater fronts or armhole openings, and the cut edges are secured by one of several methods.

To make a vertical opening, knitters have long used a technique called steeking, which leaves a band of unknit strands. To make steeks, yarn over seven times where you want the opening, as in the drawing on the facing page. When you come to the yarn-overs on the next round, drop them off the needle and make seven more. By continuing like this, you'll form a vertical band of yarn strands that can be cut in half, leaving ends long enough to be woven into each edge of the finished garment.

With the invention of the sewing machine in the 19th century, knitters began to use machine stitching as a way of safely handling cut ends of yarn. After knitting the tube, the knitter makes two rows of straight machine stitching, one on top of the other, on either side of the vertical row of stitches to be cut (see drawing, facing page). This stitching firmly fastens the yarn ends, preventing them from raveling. The cut edges are then hidden in a seam or covered with crochet.

Maggie Righetti, of Atlanta, GA, is a knitting designer and teacher and the author of Universal Yarn Finder.

Knitters of multicolored patterns have traditionally carried the yarn in both hands. The knitter carries the dominant color of a particular round in the right hand and works the stitches of that color in the American-British style, wrapping the yarn around the right needle with the right hand. The knitter carries the less often used color or colors in the left hand and knits them in the Continental style, using the right needle to scoop up the yarn that runs over the left forefinger, as shown in the photo on the facing page. If the left hand carries more than one yarn, the knitter simply picks off the needed color. Since all the yarns are carried along as the knitting progresses, it isn't necessary to drop one color and pick up another, as it is when only the American-British style of knitting is used. It's beautiful to see an accomplished knitter effortlessly making stitches, first with the right yarn, then with the left yarn.

To knit a Fair Isle or Nordic sweater in the round, you need to know how to work only knit stitches in the Continental style, since knitting in the round eliminates purling. Insert the right needle into the stitch in the usual way. Keep your left hand motionless and from right to left scoop up the strand from your left forefinger.

In traditional multicolored designs there are rarely more than five stitches between color repeats, so there are no long yarn floats on the underside of the garment. However, some new patterns do include long spaces between colors. This makes it necessary for the knitter to "catch" the floating yarn every fourth or fifth stitch. Catching the yarn is easiest when you are knitting in the Continental style. (This is why the least used yarns are held in the left hand.) After inserting the needle to make a stitch with the working yarn, lay the yarn to be caught over the right needle, as shown in the drawing on the facing page. Form the stitch in the usual manner *under* the caught strand, without incorporating it into the stitch itself.

If a design requires that you catch strands often, choose your colors carefully. A shadow of color will inevitably show through on the knit side wherever yarn has been caught. As long as the caught color is of a lighter hue and intensity than the background color, it won't be obvious. But beware of making a garment with a white background and frequently catching dark-colored strands, as it will look messy.

It's obvious why knitters of traditional ethnic patterns choose to work in the round. First, it is easier to follow complex charts with the right side of the work always facing the knitter. This eliminates the need to read the chart backward and work the pattern with purl stitches. Second, it is easier to catch strands from the knit, rather than the purl, position. Third, working in the round makes it easier to knit in the Continental style, which in turn eliminates the need to drop and pick up yarns when colors are changed.

Unfortunately, many contemporary Fair Isle and Nordic patterns are designed in flat pieces rather than in the round. But you can easily change instructions for a flat sweater to work it in the round. Add together all the stitches across the back and front of the pattern. Look at the chart of the design to see if any stitches were added for seams. If stitches were added, subtract them so that the garment will not be too big.

Fair Isle and Nordic garments are rewarding both to make and to wear. Understanding the easy, traditional way to produce the designs should encourage you to make many of them—happily and confidently working in the round. □

To knit in the Continental style, carry the yarn on your left forefinger (blue yarn in photo), and insert the needle into the stitch in the usual way. Scoop up the yarn with the right needle, and pull it through as usual. The dominant color in the row (yellow yarn) is held in the right hand.

From *Threads* magazine (August 1986) 6:40-41

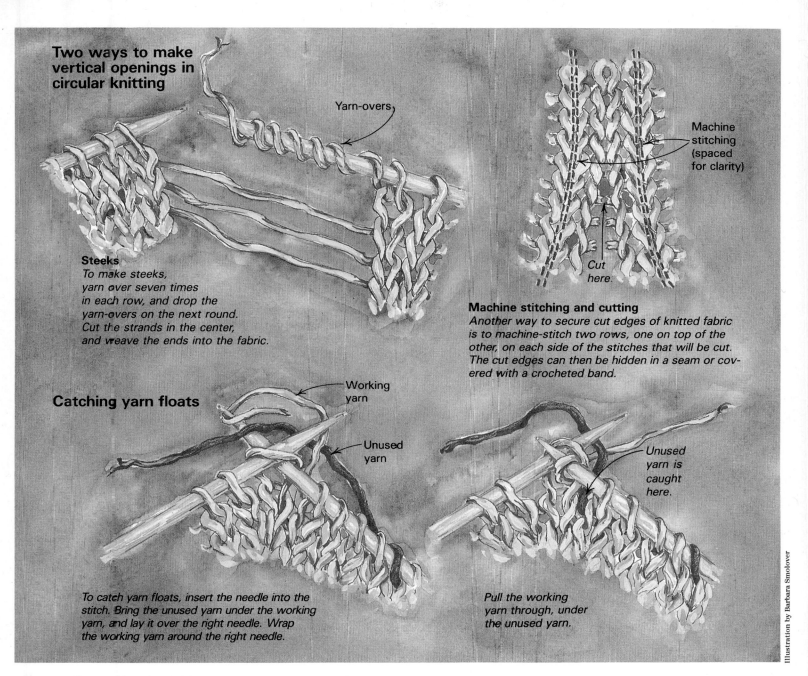

Two ways to make vertical openings in circular knitting

Yarn-overs

Steeks
To make steeks,
yarn over seven times
in each row, and drop the
yarn-overs on the next round.
Cut the strands in the center,
and weave the ends into the fabric.

Machine stitching (spaced for clarity)

Cut here.

Machine stitching and cutting
Another way to secure cut edges of knitted fabric is to machine-stitch two rows, one on top of the other, on each side of the stitches that will be cut. The cut edges can then be hidden in a seam or covered with a crocheted band.

Catching yarn floats

Working yarn

Unused yarn

To catch yarn floats, insert the needle into the stitch. Bring the unused yarn under the working yarn, and lay it over the right needle. Wrap the working yarn around the right needle.

Unused yarn is caught here.

Pull the working yarn through, under the unused yarn.

Illustration by Barbara Smolover

Knit Paintings

Beyond glorious color with Japanese knitting techniques

by Yoshimi Kihara

Knitting is a handicraft. Its greatest challenge is in using your hands to create a work that corresponds to the image you have in your imagination. Ironically, in the process of making samples and finished garments, we often discover new and better ideas than our original conceptions. My development has carried on this way—passing from my preconceived idea to actual result; and gradually, I've learned how to chart the route in between. It is a road down which I am still traveling.

Designing a sweater

I believe that designing knitwear can be approached from opposite directions. On the one hand, you can imagine the complete garment in three dimensions, taking into account its function on the human body with its movements and stresses. In this case, you proceed from the whole to its parts. Or you can concentrate on surface design and patterns, creating a cloth. This way you're working from the details toward the whole. Ideally, of course, you should aim for a synthesis in both directions. Certainly, when we make wearable clothes, we can't ignore such practical elements as general comfort, washability, etc. There is always a balance between possibilities and limitations imposed by the requirement that the garment be wearable.

When I began designing, I worked from the whole to the parts; but over the past five or six years, as my patterns grew more complex and the number of colors and yarns more numerous, I gradually moved toward a focus on the cloth. Although I try to keep in mind the wider viewpoint, I often find myself getting bogged down in detail or repeating some part of my idea over and over. In a sense, this is part of forming one's own style. Through long trial and experiment, we settle on certain ways of balancing colors and shapes or of using techniques that contribute to our own individual aesthetic. Unfortunately, it is so much easier to stay with the tried and tested methods than to face a new challenge again from start to finish.

Most of my designs have been based on geometric patterns, like the sweater at right on the facing page (pattern on p. 48); but I also enjoy working with abstract shapes, like those in the sweater shown at left, facing page. I usually begin with rough outline sketches, exploring rhythm and colors. Later I translate the sketch onto graph paper with one square equaling one stitch and two rows, as shown in the large chart on p. 49. Occasionally, however, I begin by making a life drawing, and sometimes I try to draw directly onto graph paper from a "life" source such as the flowers in my garden.

Next, using the graph paper, I decide the precise balance of line and shape and which colors and materials will work most effectively with the design. My present interest is in using warmer colors in small quantities to add small emotional hints to my rather cool-hearted patterns.

I use yarns with varying surface characteristics: mohair, angora, wool, silk, tweed, and bouclé, for example, to produce relief effects that form a counter-rhythm to that of the color and surface geometry.

Unfortunately, I have had no formal art or design education, and although this article and my finished work may give the impression that it is all plain sailing, it isn't. Often my designs are not as successful as I'd hoped. At first when I made a very complicated sweater, I knew I couldn't repeat it, but I'd make myself do it again anyway. This way, I could correct any problems, and I also mastered the skills I'd just begun to develop with the first sweater. Then I could go on to the next level of complication and even finer design.

Writing the pattern

Before starting to knit, I always work out the knitting gauge and overall shape. There is no one "best" knitting technique. I use intarsia, stranding, and weaving-in. I believe that the most effective methods are often those we are most familiar with already. My one rule is that there are never any floats.

I use the Japanese method to design my garments. This is similar to dressmaking techniques. To determine the shape of the clothing pieces, I scale down to a fourth or a fifth of the actual size for convenience and draw the outline of the shapes on graph paper. Then, using my gauge, I can calculate the number of stitches and rows in each knitted piece.

My fabric is mostly stockinette, but I usually use lines or areas of purl stitches for accent and texture. Each type of stitch is indicated by its own symbol on the graphed pattern, which also includes symbols that indicate the technical methods to be used, such as "knit two together." Japanese patterns show us instantly not only the garment's structure, but also exactly how to knit it. If you look at the pattern on p. 48, you'll see that it is like a blueprint for the garment's architecture. And by coloring the squares of the graph paper, I can add that level of instruction as well.

If you're new to this method, it is useful to draw the exact size of each piece on large paper, in addition to drawing the scaled-down size. While you are knitting, you can put your work on top of the exact shape to make sure you are going in the right direction. When you finish the sweater, try it on to check for comfort so you can work out improvements for your next paper pattern.

Keep your patterns in a file, and build up a record of your design experiences. Having the graphed paper patterns allows you to analyze what you've done. Sometimes I

Working from carefully charted abstract and geometric designs, Yoshimi Kihara makes effortless-looking transitions between dozens of colors and fibers. The author explains some of her special tricks; and as you knit the sweater at far right (pattern on p. 48), you'll also learn how to use Japanese-style patterns. (Photo by Yvonne Taylor)

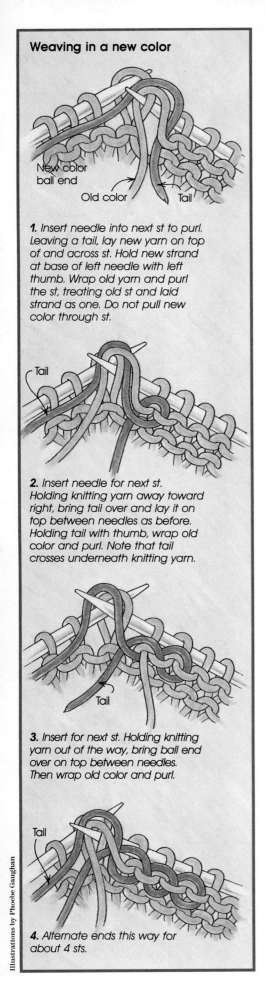

1. Insert needle into next st to purl. Leaving a tail, lay new yarn on top of and across st. Hold new strand at base of left needle with left thumb. Wrap old yarn and purl the st, treating old st and laid strand as one. Do not pull new color through st.

2. Insert needle for next st. Holding knitting yarn away toward right, bring tail over and lay it on top between needles as before. Holding tail with thumb, wrap old color and purl. Note that tail crosses underneath knitting yarn.

3. Insert for next st. Holding knitting yarn out of the way, bring ball end over on top between needles. Then wrap old color and purl.

4. Alternate ends this way for about 4 sts.

Illustrations by Phoebe Gaughan

begin a new work using a previous pattern that I alter slightly and rearrange as I knit. Thinking about my old patterns makes it fun to change and improve them.

Handling many colors as you knit

Almost all the yarns I use are a single color, although sometimes my sweaters look as though I knit them with space-dyed yarns. I get this effect, the gradual shading of the pattern sweater on p. 45, and my watercolor painting look by making frequent color changes over few stitches.

I use a variety of methods for working with color in all my work—depending on which technique is most logical in a particular area of the knitting. I work with whole balls of yarn rather than short pieces. To keep the balls from becoming hopelessly tangled, I have a special trick for turning my work over. When I finish the right side row, I turn the full needle toward the left to put the wrong side up. When I finish the wrong side row, I turn the full needle back toward the right. By turning the work first one way and then the other consistently, the balls of yarn always return to their original untwisted positions.

If there will be large areas of a single color, I work them in intarsia, but since I usually use many colors all over the piece with just a few stitches of each at a time, the technique I use most frequently is stranding, holding one color in each hand, and weaving in the strands every other stitch by wrapping them behind the running yarn to prevent floats. (Note: You can find drawings and a description of the basic weaving-in technique on pp. 106-108 of *Mary Thomas's Knitting Book* [Dover Publications, Inc., 1972].)

To make my sweaters as neat and almost as beautiful on the wrong side as on the right side (see the detail on the facing page), I wrap, or weave, the colors I will be using into position on the row before I need them if they need to move two or more stitches. This means that I must keep a close eye on my chart and prepare for every color change ahead of time. Usually I attach the chart to the wall next to my knitting chair so I can see it at a glance. My wrapping technique makes it easier for me to work with lots of colors. Since wrapping thickens the fabric, using many colors gives my sweaters a consistent weight and texture. I try not to weave in too many yarns in the same place so the work doesn't get too thick.

Starting and ending a color—Sometimes, I start a color right before using it; but to ensure that I won't have too many ends to finish by hand when the sweater is completed, I try to start new colors the row before I'll want them about four stitches ear-

ly. On the purl side, I weave the strand and its tail into position, as shown in the drawings at left. You can also do this on the knit side. Two alternations gives a firm enough join, but four is stronger and more solid, and you won't have to needle-weave the tail later. Wrapping in ends this way thickens the row, so you need to spread out your color additions across the row. Since the yarns can show through a little, I always try to join dark colors in dark areas.

I finish off a color by wrapping and alternating the ends almost exactly the same way. But at stress points like the elbow, I finish off colors over more than two rows.

Changing colors—When I'm moving a color to a new area, I position it one stitch beyond where it will be used on the next row. For example, if I need to move the yarn across six stitches, I travel seven, wrapping the yarn every few stitches. Going one extra stitch means I won't have to twist the strands to prevent a hole when I change them. It is easier to move colors toward the left on the knit side every other row since that's the direction the knitting moves, but you can move them in either direction every row with careful preparation on the previous row or rows.

Whether I'm knitting or purling, I prepare for each color change one stitch ahead by wrapping the new color yarn into the old color stitch using the technique Mary Thomas shows for weaving in the yarn held in the left hand. Since I prefer Continental knitting, the old color is already in my left hand. On the knit side, since the yarn is in back, I also hold the new color between my left thumb and middle finger while I wrap it. I work the next stitch in the new color. But when I wrap a new color on the purl side, I hold it in my right hand because the yarn is in front and can't be picked.

Although this technique keeps the knitting even, firm, and without gaps, and allows you to move colors freely without tangling, it has some minor disadvantages. First, on the knit side, it slightly raises the old color stitch at the wrap. Second, if you wrap too tightly, the stitch will be without stretch. Third, you can only do this if the wrapped stitch is stocking stitch on the front. If you want a purl stitch at the change, you must twist the yarns. Twisting is also the better technique for a vertical stripe.

Finishing tips

I usually work with lightweight yarns, but when using heavy or bulky yarns it's a good idea to plan bind-offs carefully and sew seams with a modified backstitch to prevent stretching. Normally I bind off on the wrong side a little loosely, using a needle one size bigger. Since binding off steadies knitting and prevents stretching, I usually bind off the back neck and shoulders to help the garment keep its shape. But binding off adds bulk, so I often leave the front stitches live and sew them to the back bind-off, as shown in the top drawing at right. This makes a seam that is less bulky but has lots of stability so a heavy sleeve won't pull the shoulder down.

When I sew two bound-off edges together, I backstitch with a length of yarn about three times the seam length. If the fabric is thick, I insert the needle just below both bars of the chain at the top of the bind-off on both pieces of knitting, as shown in the lower drawing at near right. If the fabric is thinner, I can make a prettier seam by backstitching through the last row of stitches before the bind-off, as shown at far right.

Even though I weave in my colors as I knit, I always have a few ends to finish off at the bind-off edges. I sew each end into the bind-off bars two or three stitches, then backstitch and repeat. The backstitch is very, very important, and two are stronger than one. I may have as many as four yarns to finish off in the same place (especially where shoulders and sleeves meet). To avoid going into the same place too often, I sew into other bind-off seams or into the other side of the bind-off edge.

I like to line my sweaters, especially the cardigans. But that's another story.

Suggestions for knitting the pattern

My sweater jacket, shown at right, p. 45 (pattern on p. 48), is suitable for almost any competent knitter. If you are new to these techniques, you can work it with only two or three colors and yarns as you learn how to add and move them. More advanced knitters will enjoy changing colors often to produce the gradation effect. I hope you'll choose and arrange your own colors, perhaps dyeing them yourself. I knit the first jacket in two fibers, mohair (M) and wool (W), each in dark gray (300 yd. M, 180 yd. W); medium gray (260 yd. M, 200 yd. W); light gray (260 yd. M, 200 yd. W); pale gray or off-white (250 yd. M, 100 yd. W); and white (300 yd. M, 280 yd. W); as well as in black wool (150 yd.). The second time, I used silk instead of wool, which I think looks better. I also changed the way I graded the colors (see the chart on p. 49) to increase their subtlety. I would very much enjoy seeing slides of your creations. You can mail them to me at 181 Fillebrook Rd., London E11 1AF, England. ⇨

Yoshimi Kihara of London, England, designs hand- and machine-knit sweater patterns for Hamanaka Co., Ltd. N. R. (Mr. Tanigawa), 2-3, Yabunoshita-chō, Hanazono, Ukyo-ku, Kyoto-city, Japan. She sometimes sells her one-of-a-kind garments in select stores internationally.

Meticulous wrapping and advanced preparation for each color addition produces a sweater that's almost as beautiful and subtle on the inside as on the outside.

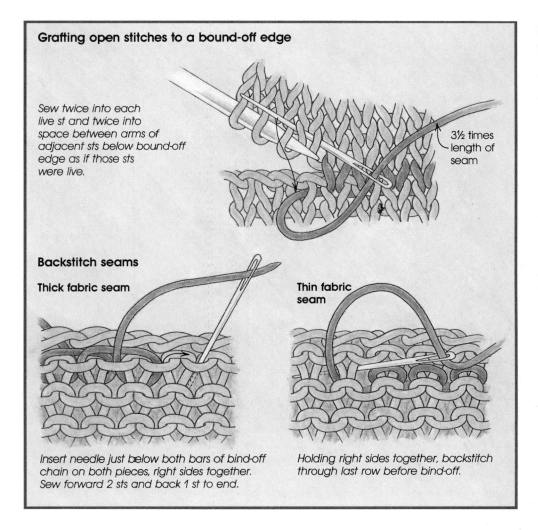

Grafting open stitches to a bound-off edge

Sew twice into each live st and twice into space between arms of adjacent sts below bound-off edge as if those sts were live.

3½ times length of seam

Backstitch seams

Thick fabric seam

Insert needle just below both bars of bind-off chain on both pieces, right sides together. Sew forward 2 sts and back 1 st to end.

Thin fabric seam

Holding right sides together, backstitch through last row before bind-off.

Yoshimi Kihara's Shaded Zigzag Jacket

Red lines indicate front; blue outlines indicate back.

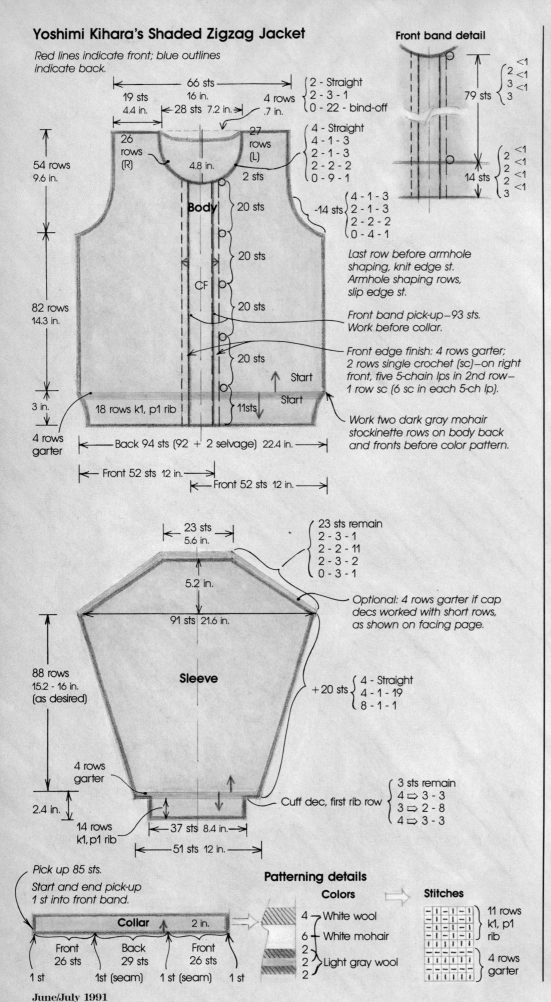

Front band detail

Body

CF

Start
Start

2 - Straight
2 - 3 - 1
0 - 22 - bind-off

4 - Straight
4 - 1 - 3
2 - 1 - 3
2 - 2 - 2
0 - 9 - 1

4 - 1 - 3
2 - 1 - 3
2 - 2 - 2
0 - 4 - 1

66 sts
16 in.
19 sts
4.4 in.
28 sts 7.2 in.
4 rows
.7 in.

26 rows (R)
27 rows (L)
4.8 in.

54 rows
9.6 in.

82 rows
14.3 in.

3 in.

4 rows garter

79 sts
14 sts

2 <1
3 <1
3

2 <1
2 <1
2 <1
3 <1

20 sts
20 sts
20 sts
20 sts
-14 sts
11 sts
2 sts

Last row before armhole shaping, knit edge st. Armhole shaping rows, slip edge st.

Front band pick-up—93 sts. Work before collar.

Front edge finish: 4 rows garter; 2 rows single crochet (sc)—on right front, five 5-chain lps in 2nd row—1 row sc (6 sc in each 5-ch lp).

Work two dark gray mohair stockinette rows on body back and fronts before color pattern.

18 rows k1, p1 rib

Back 94 sts (92 + 2 selvage) 22.4 in.

Front 52 sts 12 in.

Front 52 sts 12 in.

Sleeve

23 sts
5.6 in.

5.2 in.

91 sts 21.6 in.

88 rows
15.2 - 16 in.
(as desired)

4 rows garter

2.4 in.

14 rows k1, p1 rib

37 sts 8.4 in.

51 sts 12 in.

23 sts remain
2 - 3 - 1
2 - 2 - 11
2 - 3 - 2
0 - 3 - 1

Optional: 4 rows garter if cap decs worked with short rows, as shown on facing page.

+ 20 sts
4 - Straight
4 - 1 - 19
8 - 1 - 1

3 sts remain
4 ⇒ 3 - 3
3 ⇒ 2 - 8
4 ⇒ 3 - 3

Cuff dec, first rib row

Pick up 85 sts.
Start and end pick-up 1 st into front band.

Collar 2 in.

Front 26 sts
Back 29 sts
Front 26 sts

1st
1st (seam)
1st (seam)
1st

Patterning details

Colors

4 — White wool
6 — White mohair
2
2
2
2 — Light gray wool

Stitches

11 rows k1, p1 rib

4 rows garter

June/July 1991

Size and materials

Gauge: 4 in. = 16.5 sts by 23 rows on 5mm needles (US size 8); or size needed to obtain gauge.

Yarns: Mohair in standard weight, approx. 1,370 yd. Wool, silk, or blend; 3-ply weight, approx. 1,030 yd. We used Telana dye from Cerulean Blue (PO Box 21168, Seattle, WA 98111-3168; 206-323-8600) to dye "Toaga" mohair and "Silk and Ivory" 50% wool/50% silk from Henry's Attic (5 Mercury Ave., Monroe, NY 10950; 914-783-3930 for your nearest retailer).—Eds.

Size: Finished bust, 45 in.

General techniques

Red arrows on piece schematics indicate direction of working.

Work shaping symmetrically; i.e., on back and sleeves apply directions twice, once for each side.

Use crochet provisional cast-on (see Basics, Threads No. 35, pp. 18 and 20) to cast on for sweater pieces. Pick up and knit ribbings from cast-on edge. bind off ribbings using tubular cast-off (see drawing at far right).

Shaping and pick-up notations:

*Japanese patterns indicate increase and decrease frequency and pick-up ratios with a telegraphic series of numbers. Dashes, arrows, or carets between the numbers symbolize the operation. You can bind off or decrease for single decrease stitches, as you prefer. **Read all of these shaping charts from the bottom up and left to right.***

0 = first row of shaping.

Shaping

Every x Row - Dec/Inc x Sts - x Times.

For example, read:
4 - Straight
4 - 1 - 3
2 - 1 - 3
2 - 2 - 2
0 - 9 - 1
as:
1. First row, bind off 9 sts, once.
2. Every 2nd row, bind off 2 sts, twice.
3. Every 2nd row, dec 1 st, three times.
4. Every 4th row, dec 1 st, three times.
5. Work 4 rows straight.

Pick-up (front band)

Read:

<1
3

as: Pick up a st at selvage in every row 3 times, skip (<) 1 row, and so on, to top of column. Repeat series for required number of sts.

Decreasing evenly across row (sleeve, cuff)

Knit St x ⇒ (together with) St x - x Times.

For example: Knit 4th st tog with 3rd st, 3 times; then 3rd st tog with 2nd st, 8 times; etc., across one row.

Color and stitch patterns

Zigzag pattern for body and sleeves

On chart, 1 square = 1 st and 2 rows. Read right to left, bottom to top.

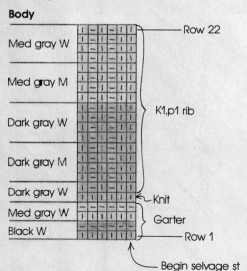

Begin sleeve

Begin back and fronts.

14-st repeat

7 rows
17 rows
7 rows
33 rows

Key

☐ or ⌶	Knit (RS); Purl (WS)
⊟	Purl (RS); Knit (WS)
⊠	Knit 2 sts tog
☐	Mohair
▨	Wool
▨	Black
▨	Dark gray
☐	Med gray
☐	Lt gray
☐	White

For graded colors, work first 33 rows grading zigzag as shown. Grade mohair base over next 7 rows; then grade zigzag in next 17 rows. Repeat 7 row and 17 row, grading patterns in progressively lighter colors to end of piece. Last portion will be all white.

Work 2-st zigzags in wool or silk, every other one in white. Work 5-st zigzags in mohair.

For simpler color pattern, use 3 yarns: White for alternate 2-st wool zigzags; second color for other wool zigzags and mohair base.

Tubular cast-off

To begin, work 2 rows tubular stockinette: When row begins with a k st, *k1, sl 1 pwise with yarn in front (wyif).* When row begins with a p st, *sl 1 pwise wyif, k1. Cut yarn 3 to 4 times length of seam.

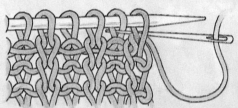

1. First 2 sts: Insert tapestry needle pwise into first k st and kwise from behind into first p st. Leave both sts on needle. **Always work with tapestry needle below knitting needle.**

2. Pair of knit sts: Insert needle kwise into first k st, and drop it. Then go pwise into 2nd k st; pull yarn through.

3. Pair of purl sts: Go pwise into first p st, and drop it. Loop yarn to right and under knitting needle, and insert tapestry needle kwise from behind into second p st. Pull yarn through.

Repeat pairs of k sts and pairs of p sts to end of row, remembering to drop st only after needle has passed through it twice.

Ribbing colors/yarns/pattern

W = wool; M = mohair.   1 Square = 1 st/1 row.

Body

Row 22

Med gray W

Med gray M

K1,p1 rib

Dark gray W

Dark gray M

Dark gray W — Knit

Med gray W — Garter

Black W — Row 1

— Begin selvage st

Sleeve

Row 18

Med gray W

Med gray M

k1,p1 rib

Dark gray M

Dark gray W — Knit, dec row

Med gray W — Garter

Black W — Row 1

— Begin selvage st

End selvage st

Short rowing for sleeve cap

Instead of decreasing, work progressively shorter rows, turning before each dec st. End with all sts on needle. Work 4 rows garter over entire cap.

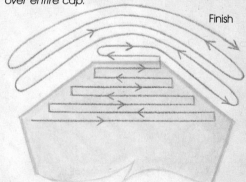

Finish

Cut yarn 3½ times length of seam and graft cap to armhole using method shown on p. 47.

Swedish Two-Strand Knitting

Decorative double-thick fabric from both ends of the ball

by Linda D. Y. Sokalski

Mittens and gloves are the most common application for tvåändsstickning. Linda Sokalski's mittens are fun to knit because of the variety of crooked-stitch designs (the pattern is on p. 54). In true Swedish style, the mittens aren't interchangeable, as the thumb gusset is formed on one side only, and the back of the hand is patterned.

*d*alarna Province, in the heart of Sweden, is a striking contrast to the modern, progressive image we generally associate with Scandinavia. It is here that a most unusual knitting technique quite unlike anything encountered in any other part of the world is still practiced and taught. The technique is called *tvåändsstickning* (tvo'-ends-stick'-ning, literally two ends knitting). To do it, you continually twist two strands of yarn around each other, forming alternating stitches. The reverse side resembles crocheted afghan stitch, and the fabric is dense and airtight, perfect for cold Swedish winters. The density, as well as the absence of long floats, also contributes to durability.

While on a business trip to Sweden a few years ago, I was introduced to *tvåändsstickning* at the Stockholm Handcraft Guild. Among the books I acquired, *Tvåändsstickat*, published in 1984 by the Dalarnas Museum, is probably the most comprehensive. I'm sorry the English translation wasn't available then (*Twined Knitting*, 1989, by Birgitta Dandanell and Ulla Danielsson, Interweave Press, 306 N. Washington Ave., Loveland, CO 80537; $18.95 + $2.50 S&H). It would have saved a lot of confusion when I tried to teach myself the technique with only the photos and drawings as guides. A picture may be worth a thousand words, but a picture with a few words of explanation is probably worth ten thousand. I also assumed the accuracy of two English references that asserted you could achieve the same effect much more easily by stranding, where one strand is always above the other. This technique will yield different results, depending on the number of stitches being odd or even, but it isn't *tvåändsstickning*. To convince myself I was doing it right, and to learn more, I eventually spent a week at Sätergläntan, a craft school in Dalarna.

Your initial reaction to the correct technique may be like mine. You may wonder if the effort of continually twisting the yarn is worth it. But if you persevere, completing the mittens in the photo at left (pattern on p. 54), you're likely to become as obsessed as I am with this unique and fascinating technique.

Background—*Tvåändsstickning* had been largely forgotten in the 20th century until 1974, when an archaeological investigation in the old copper mining town, Falun, produced a glove so interesting that it inspired extensive research. Initially, it was thought that the glove, made before 1680, could have been worked in *nålbinding*, a type of needle lace common to Scandinavia since the Iron Age. Closer investigation, however, indicated it was knit in *tvåändsstickning*, the only knitting technique known to the peasant population of Dalarna by the middle of the 1600s. Because there were many immigrants at that time, one historian, Inga Wintzell, postulates that the technique may have originated in Germany. The technique is also known in bordering areas of Norway, where coarse gloves are worked with the wrong side out. The warmth is often increased by pile, which is sewn through the horizontal stripes.

Despite its lack of popularity during most of this century, *tvåändsstickning* never fell into disuse in Sollerön, an island in Lake Siljan. Sollerön is particularly known for elaborately patterned gloves and stockings using *krokmaskor*, textured surface patterns. Gloves were usually worked in white cotton and were made for weddings—fingerless gloves for the bride and finger gloves for the bridegroom. Lima parish, on the Norwegian border, is also known for wedding gloves dating from the 1800s. The pattern was generally plain—at most a border pattern and usually some marking of the thumb gusset. What is remarkable about these gloves is their fineness—the gauge was typically 23 sts/in.

While the origin of *tvåändsstickning* is unknown, its decline is well documented. *Tvåändsstickning* was always done with the yarn held in the right hand and thrown. In the 1860s, however, Eilert Sundt, a Norwegian sociologist, issued a report that "proved" knitting could be done faster with the yarn held in the left hand. Around the same period, knitting began to be taught in the elementary schools, and the left-hand technique was taught as the "correct" method. There are still some older women around who recount the difficulty of learning the school method after having learned the old method at home. Sundt's studies never considered *tvåändsstickning*, which also was not included in the school curriculum and thus fell into disuse.

Yarn and needles—*Tvåändsstickning* is usually worked in the round on double-pointed needles with fine yarn. European double-pointeds come in sets of five instead of four, and patterns like the pattern on p. 54 are written accordingly. It's assumed that there are equal numbers of stitches on each needle unless the pattern states otherwise.

Older pieces were most often knit in wool, but linen and cotton are also found. Wool yarn was sometimes blended with rabbit hair to obtain a whiter color or with dog hair to be more waterproof. Since textured surface patterns show up best in white, it was the most popular color, often with red trim. Black was also used frequently, and sometimes various shades of green. In Norway, coarser work was done in natural gray. Today, it's also very popular to use one strand of white with one strand of gray to create striped fabric, but white remains the most common color.

Traditional Swedish yarns tend to be firmer and less elastic than most of our wool yarns, but fingering or sport-weight wool is suitable for *tvåändsstickning*. Worsted-weight yarn is too heavy for most garments.

Before you begin knitting, roll the yarn into a ball that feeds from both the inside and outside—thus the two ends. When the yarn becomes excessively twisted, pin the two ends to the ball with a knitting needle, as shown in the drawing below, and let the ball spin to untwist them.

Most of the yarns we buy today are S-plied. The twisting motion of *tvåändsstickning* will twist these yarns tighter, and it will sometimes feel as if the yarn is fighting back. Examination of old pieces disclosed that they were often done with Z-plied yarn, which untwists as it's knit. A special Z-plied yarn is made for *tvåändsstickning* by Wåhlstedts Textilverkstad, Box 731, 780 44 DALA-FLODA, Sweden. It's available in white and natural black for 55 crowns (about $8) for 100 g. A sample card is 35 crowns ($5).

Working in *tvåändsstickning*—Traditional application of *tvåändsstickning* is generally limited to mittens and gloves (the most common), stockings and socks, and sleeves. Occasionally sweaters are worked in *tvåändsstickning*, but caps rarely are.

Since Swedish mittens are usually made very large to allow air circulation for warmth, there are a number of shaping variations. Older patterns didn't use ribbing at the cuff. The mittens were knit straight or with a gauntlet to fit over the sleeve cuff. The decreases at the fingertips and thumb or at the top of a mitten are always at the sides rather than evenly spaced. And because of the way the shaping is done, the two hands are worked as mirror images.

In general, the thumb gusset lies on the palm side of the glove, rather than at the

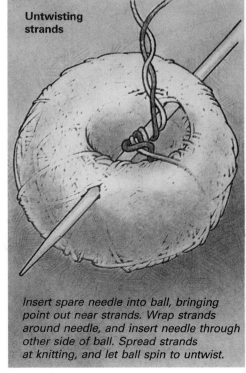

Untwisting strands

Insert spare needle into ball, bringing point out near strands. Wrap strands around needle, and insert needle through other side of ball. Spread strands at knitting, and let ball spin to untwist.

Illustrations by Clarke

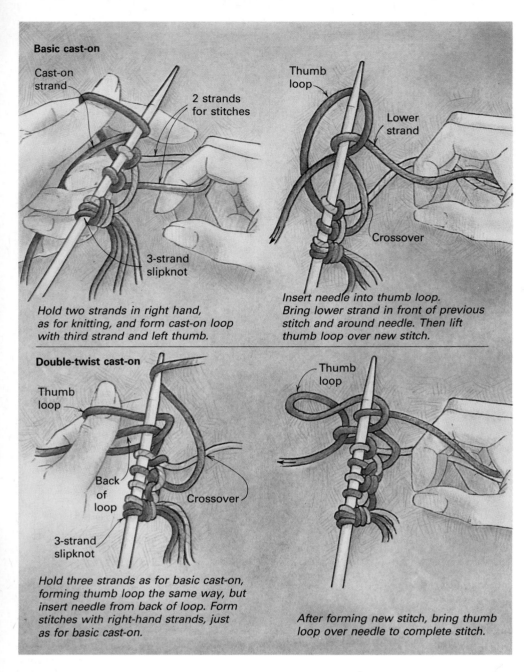

Basic cast-on

Cast-on strand

2 strands for stitches

3-strand slipknot

Hold two strands in right hand, as for knitting, and form cast-on loop with third strand and left thumb.

Thumb loop

Lower strand

Crossover

Insert needle into thumb loop. Bring lower strand in front of previous stitch and around needle. Then lift thumb loop over new stitch.

Double-twist cast-on

Thumb loop

Back of loop

Crossover

3-strand slipknot

Hold three strands as for basic cast-on, forming thumb loop the same way, but insert needle from back of loop. Form stitches with right-hand strands, just as for basic cast-on.

Thumb loop

After forming new stitch, bring thumb loop over needle to complete stitch.

side. The simplest gusset has no shaping at all. When you're ready to separate for the thumb, you put half the required number of stitches on a holder and cast on an identical number. Formerly, a mittten was often knit without a thumb. After the body was completed, the knitter would cut the opening at the proper position and pick out the correct number of stitches. She picked up stitches along both sides and knit the thumb to the proper length. (See "Afterthought pockets" in the article by Meg Swansen on p. 83.) This unshaped thumb opening works largely because of the loose fit.

Shaped gussets can have increases along both sides or at the center. One of the most common has increases along one side only (see pattern, p. 54).

The basic technique—The way you hold the yarn and the way you use your right hand differ greatly from the methods used in ordinary knitting. At first, *tvåändsstickning* may seem awkward, especially if you're used to holding the yarn in your left hand. But with practice you'll find it more comfortable, and the knitting will go more quickly.

To knit, hold the yarn in your right hand, one strand in front of (or below) your index finger and the other between your middle fingers. Pick up the strand below your index finger by tilting your index finger into position, and use it to knit the next stitch (photo at top right, facing page), which results in a half-twist of the two strands. Then insert your index finger between the strands (photo at left, facing page), followed by your middle finger, to return to the starting position. Repeat this process with each stitch, each time lifting the strand under the index finger forward over the strand used for the previous stitch.

For reverse (purl) rows, both strands are on the front, and the new strand is brought under the strand previously worked (photo at bottom right, facing page). Although the motion seems to be in the opposite direction, you're still twisting the yarn around the previously worked strand in a clockwise direction. Since *tvåändsstickning* is usually worked in the round, reverse rows are used mainly for decorative effects (see top of mitten cuff on pp. 50 and 54 and in photo at left). You can also work a reverse row after casting on to help prevent the edge from curling, but it's easier to do this if you work a knit row on the wrong side before joining the round.

Casting on for *tvåändsstickning* is similar to the common two-tail or double cast-on, but you use three strands instead of two, typically one strand of red and two strands of white. Start with a large slipknot with all three strands. (You'll drop this knot off without knitting it at the end of the first row, before joining the round.) Hold the red strand in your left hand and the two white strands in your right, in the same

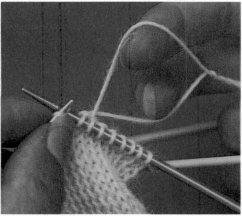

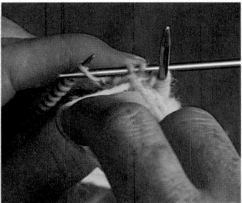

To twist strands for the next knit stitch, slip your index finger under the strand you just knit and scoop the back strand forward (photo above). Replace your second finger between the repositioned strands and knit with the strand in front of your index finger (top photo, right).

Purl, holding both strands in front. Bring the strand to be purled under the one just worked, and wrap the yarn as a normal purl stitch.

manner as for knitting. Form a half-twist loop with your left thumb (drawing at top left, facing page), and insert the needle. Wrap the first white strand around the tip of the needle and pass the loop over it (drawing at top right, facing page). Repeat, using the second white strand. Continue like this, each time bringing the new white strand forward over the one used to cast on the previous stitch, in the same manner as for knitting. The strands will twist.

A variation of this technique, sometimes called the *double-twist cast-on,* involves a full twist of the left-hand loop rather than a half-twist. After forming the loop with your left thumb, insert the needle from the back, under the thumb (drawing at lower left, facing page). Treat the two strands in your right hand in exactly the same way as with the basic cast-on method. Pass the red loop over the stitch (drawing at lower right, facing page). This cast-on is not only very decorative, but it also results in a more elastic edge, which is particularly suitable for cotton and linen yarns.

After casting on, you generally work two rows before joining the round. The first row, which is a wrong-side row, adds a decorative ridge if you knit it. Working it in two colors gives the appearance of a twisted cord. The second row is a right-side row, which you must complete before joining so you'll be working in the right direction.

Increasing in *tvåändsstickning* is remarkably simple and relatively invisible.

Since there are two strands of working yarn, you just work a stitch twice—once with each strand in the same side of the stitch, always continuing to twist them. Double increases, i.e., 3 sts in 1 st, are unknown. But if it were necessary, you'd make single increases in adjacent stitches.

Decreases are worked as in plain knitting, either right hand (k2tog) or left hand (sl1-k1-psso or SSK).

Embellishment of *tvåändsstickning* falls into three basic categories: embroidery, multicolor knitting, and textured patterns, known collectively as *ytmönster* (literally, surface patterns). Often all three were combined in the same garment. I'll concentrate here on single-color textured patterns and follow up in my next article with multicolor work.

Surface designs, *ytmönster*— *Tvåändsstickning* is best known for its wide variety of textural surface patterns. To create these patterns, you normally bring the strand that wasn't used to work the previous stitch over the other strand and between the needles to the front. You can purl the next stitch with the front strand or knit it with the back strand. In either case, the nonworking strand is carried across the stitch (in front if you knit, behind if you purl).

The most distinctive textured pattern, unique in *tvåändsstickning,* is created with *krokmaskor* (literally, crooked stitches). Patterns generally consist of combinations of odd numbers of stitches, in which stitches

purled with the front strand and stitches knit with the back strand alternate. You leave the front strand in front until the 3, 5, etc., pattern stitches have been completed, carrying it across the alternating knit stitches. Successive rows alternate knit and purl stitches. That is, you knit the stitches you purled and purl the stitches you knit. If you work two rounds this way, the result is a chainlike pattern such as that produced on rnd 3 and rnd 4 of the mitten pattern on p. 54. The strands don't twist around each other while you work *krokmaskor.*

The design in *aviga maskor,* another type of textured pattern, consists of purl stitches. Knitting proceeds in the normal, twisted manner until you bring a strand forward for the next purl stitch. Since the strand used to purl is brought to the back of the work after each purl stitch, *aviga maskor* differs little in appearance from textured patterns created with purl stitches in normal knitting (see photo, facing page).

Krokmaskor and *aviga maskor* can be used in numerous designs. Patterns are usually geometric and appear to be adapted from weaving or pattern darning. You can work the same design, using either technique, but the effect is very different. ⇨

Linda D. Y. Sokalski of Hudson, OH, an engineer and a district manager with Ohio Bell, knits in her spare time. She pursues the byways of knitting on intensive knitting vacations.

Tvåändsstickning mitten

This mitten fits a woman who wears a size small or medium glove. Read the pattern for the right mitten from right to left; for the left mitten, read the pattern from left to right.

Materials

Brunswick Fairhaven fingering yarn, two 1-oz. balls. Any fingering yarn will do, but since the mitten should felt somewhat, use 100% wool. Shetland jumper-weight wool, knit tight, will also work. Five double-pointed needles, size 1, or size needed to obtain gauge.

Gauge

10 sts and 11 rnds = 1 in.

Sizing

The cuff pattern is a multiple of 12 sts, so you'll have to increase or decrease 6 sts on each side of the hand to knit a larger or smaller mitten. Or you can change the needle or yarn size. If you need to increase the length of the mitten at the gusset, make increases every other round (7 more rnds), or space them even more widely if necessary. For a shorter gusset, make increases every round. For a larger thumb, make more gusset increases as desired, and hold that many more thumb stitches. Increase or decrease the hand length by knitting more or fewer rounds after you've completed the back-of-hand pattern.

Key

☐ **Plain** tvåändsstickning: *Knit with both strands at back of work.*

⊡ *Purl with front strand.*

▨ *Reverse round: Purl with both strands at front.*

⊻ *Knit with back strand, carrying front strand.*

⊡⊻⊡ *Bring strand that wasn't used for previous stitch to front. Purl with front strand, knit with back strand, purl with front strand, etc. Bring front strand to back when plain stitches intervene.*

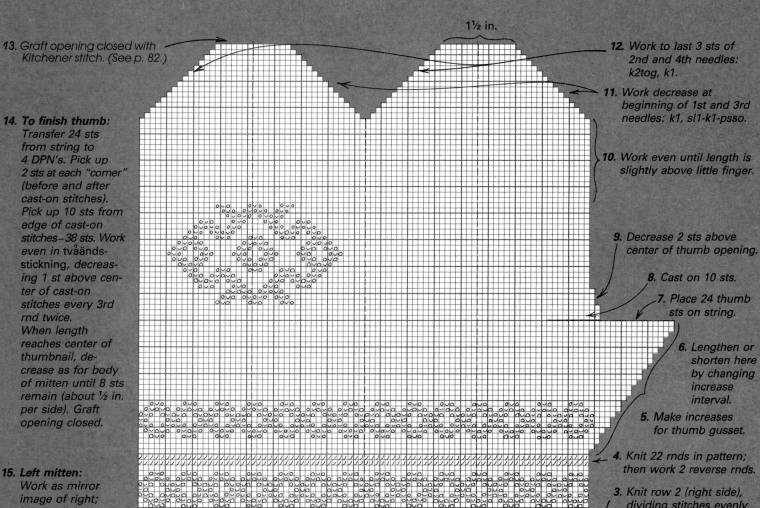

1½ in.

13. Graft opening closed with Kitchener stitch. (See p. 82.)

14. **To finish thumb:** Transfer 24 sts from string to 4 DPN's. Pick up 2 sts at each "corner" (before and after cast-on stitches). Pick up 10 sts from edge of cast-on stitches—38 sts. Work even in tvåändsstickning, decreasing 1 st above center of cast-on stitches every 3rd rnd twice. When length reaches center of thumbnail, decrease as for body of mitten until 8 sts remain (about ½ in. per side). Graft opening closed.

15. **Left mitten:** Work as mirror image of right; i.e., read chart from left to right, beginning with needle 4 (now needle 1) and ending with needle 1 (now needle 4). Form thumb gusset at end of round, rather than at beginning of round.

12. Work to last 3 sts of 2nd and 4th needles: k2tog, k1.

11. Work decrease at beginning of 1st and 3rd needles: k1, sl1-k1-psso.

10. Work even until length is slightly above little finger.

9. Decrease 2 sts above center of thumb opening.

8. Cast on 10 sts.

7. Place 24 thumb sts on string.

6. Lengthen or shorten here by changing increase interval.

5. Make increases for thumb gusset.

4. Knit 22 rnds in pattern; then work 2 reverse rnds.

3. Knit row 2 (right side), dividing stitches evenly on four needles, and join round.

2. Knit row 1 in tvåändsstickning (knit on reverse side to prevent curling. Drop cast-on slipknot at end of row.

1. Cast on 84 sts, basic method (see drawings on p. 52).

Needle 4: 21 sts   Needle 3: 21 sts   Needle 2: 21 sts   Needle 1: 21 sts

Unraveling the Myths of Shetland Lace
Learning to create openwork motifs

by Alice Starmore

a mermaid falls in love with a young Shetland fisherman, but being unable to follow him onto shore, she weaves the sea foam into a wonderful robe that enchants the islanders. They rush to copy it as closely as their resources allow.

While no one believes this legend or similar ones, the fine lace work of Shetland is surely the stuff of dreams, all too easily endowed with a touch of the supernatural. The truth, as with most human arts, is that unrelenting toil and hard-earned skill are

responsible for its existence. But the story of Shetland lace is also the story of two people, unrelated and a generation apart, who felt it their mission to assist the knitters of Shetland with almost evangelical fervor.

The Shetland lace story—Shetland, a group of over 100 islands, some only uninhabited rocks, makes up the northern limit of British soil. Because of its short growing season and wild weather, it has always relied on the sea for its livelihood. Until oil was discovered in the early 1970s, its menfolk

lived the hard life of fishermen or sailors. The women tended the croft, a small farm of about six or seven acres. Crofts provided milk, potatoes, and oatmeal, but conditions favored little else apart from the small, hardy Shetland sheep. Its wool is fine and soft and, though unsuitable for weaving, is perfect for knitting. As a result, the women of

Shetland women card wool and spin fine lace yarn. Both wear "openwork" haps (shawls) with garter-stitch centers, Old Shale borders, and Diamond edging.

From *Threads* magazine (June 1989) 23:41-45

Waves and interlocking diamonds, two rows with Bird's Eye diamonds and one row with an enlarged Shetland Fern, highlight the border of this Unst lace stole. The hexagon pattern in the center appears often.

Unst lace at its finest, this shawl combines Bird's Eye diamond edging; an elaborate diamond, wave, and tree border; and a complex center of hexagons and ferns alternated with diamonds.

Shetland have been famous as knitters since the 16th century.

Throughout the 16th, 17th, and 18th centuries, thousands of pairs of Shetland stockings were exported annually or were sold to the Continental herring fishers who worked Shetland waters in the summer. Some women sold more than their stockings to the roistering fishermen. Sir John Buchanan, Sheriff Principal of Shetland, was so affronted by what he described as "the great abominatioun and wickednes committit yeirlie" that he ordered certain huts to be burned to the ground. In the early 1800s, the Shetland hosiery trade went into decline as mechanized hosiery production increased on the British mainland.

Failure of demand caused hardship among the Shetlanders, for while fishing paid the rent, and crofting brought basic subsistence in good years, every other comfort came from spinning and knitting.

In 1838, Edward Standen, a merchant and wholesaler from Oxford, England, visited Shetland. He was impressed by some of the fine gentlemen's stockings being made there, although the knitting industry was well into its decline. He suggested that a few new products might help revitalize demand and recommended that knitters make shawls and handkerchiefs, incorporating some decorative openwork stitches. He also agreed to try to market the new products back home. The idea met with some suc-

cess, and Shetland knitters, recognizing the advantage of these innovations, adopted them eagerly. The new departure was explored, experimented with, tried, and tested; and in a few years, patterns had been pioneered, developed, and adopted. The art of Shetland lace was born. In 1844 Standen had a boating accident, which he survived, and his desire to help the islanders assumed an almost religious fervor.

He devoted his time and energy to the development and promotion of Shetland lace. He wrote pamphlets, lectured, and gathered together a collection of fine-lace articles for display in a traveling exhibition. Unfortunately, he died in 1845. Even so, he introduced to the prosperous classes of Britain what might otherwise have been destined to obscurity as a local art form.

Margaret Colvin, a native Shetlander, was the daughter of a successful commander of transatlantic steamers. She was educated in Shetland and then in Edinburgh, where she met a distinguished law student, Donald Currie, and married him at the age of 16. He died three years later, leaving her with two baby daughters, the second of whom was born while his coffin still stood in the house. A widow at 19, Margaret Currie returned to Shetland with her daughters to live with her retired father.

Life was hard for the ordinary Shetlander and had not really changed in 200 years. Fishing was dangerous, and croft work was

heavy toil for little return. The turf-roofed houses were smoky and unsanitary, and it was incredible to think that the gossamer-white Shetland shawls were produced in such dwellings. The work involved in spinning and knitting such a shawl represented about a year of hard concentration, and the Truck System, basic to the islands' economy, meant that the women saw goods in return for their labors but never received cash. The merchants made a double profit in buying a shawl. There was the profit in selling the shawl on the mainland and the profit on the goods—usually groceries or yard goods—exchanged for knitting. Widows who had no man at sea thus had no money to pay the rent. The sea gave, but it also took away, and young Shetland widows were not rarities.

Margaret Currie was in the village merchant's shop when a woman about her own age entered with a shawl that she had knit—a veritable work of art. She was offered goods in the usual way but begged to be given cash, at which the merchant made a derisory offer and told her to take it or leave it. Margaret Currie knew the woman was a widow with no cash income. She also knew that unless the low sum was accepted, the woman would have no means of paying the rent.

Currie's decision was instant—she offered the woman the full cash value of the shawl and mailed it to Lady Emma MacNeill, explaining the circumstances of its purchase. The shawl was shown to various ladies in the circle of Queen Victoria, who immediately placed orders for similar items.

The success of the small venture led Margaret Currie to use her connections to cut out the merchant middlemen and sell directly to polite Victorian society. She organized a group of knitters and took their wares for display in Edinburgh drawing rooms. Success followed success, and she extended her activities to London. She also kept up the society connection and obtained an order for 20 shawls from Queen Victoria. Through her, some Shetland knitters had royal patronage, and Shetland lace became high fashion throughout Europe.

Margaret Currie also used her influence to publicize the oppressive nature of the Truck System. A Royal Commission was constituted in 1872 to investigate the Truck System in Shetland. Despite the work of the commission, the Truck System lingered on until the 1940s.

Changes in fashion after World War I, together with mechanized lace manufacture, ended the demand for Shetland lace knitting, although the Shetland island of Unst continues a small, but steady, trade. The decline of Shetland lace was a factor in the rise of the other famous product of Shetland, Fair Isle knitting, but that's another story.

The last word in the Shetland lace story should undoubtedly be a tribute to the anonymous women of Shetland, whose skill still provides inspiration, and it is also fitting that the tribute should come from Edward Standen, who started it all. In a pamphlet published in 1844, he wrote: "The Shetland woman knits from childhood: her ball of worsted and wires accompany her everywhere—into the fields, to be taken up at intervals of rest: even during hard work she plies her industrious fingers, for she may be met on the hillside with a heavy burden on her shoulders, bending beneath the weight, but still knitting."

Techniques of lace formation—Knit lace patterns are formed by combinations of yarnovers and decreases. For those unfamiliar with lace knitting, this is often an extraordinary discovery, and it's sometimes hard to imagine how such variety and complexity can result from so few simple techniques.

Every Shetland knitter is familiar with the basic techniques of lace knitting and can, from childhood, knit all the well-known patterns, such as Old Shale, Razor Shell, and Horseshoe, which were worked on spencers (a woman's undergarment) and haps (shawls like those the spinners pictured on p. 55 are wearing). These everyday garments were worn by knitters and were also sold.

There is, however, a world of difference between an article worked in an established pattern and the fabulously elaborate designs worked on the lace pieces of Unst (photos, facing page).   See the article on p. 16. The Shetlanders make an easy distinction between the two: A simple pattern worked in normal lightweight yarn, usually with a purl wrong side, is called openwork; an elaborate design worked in very fine yarn is called lace.

Unst lace is generally worked in garter stitch to facilitate patterning on every row. This produces a very light, delicate fabric; it's less stable than that produced when yarnovers are worked on alternate rows only. Thus it requires a good deal of careful blocking when complete. Unless the yarn is extremely fine, the vertical shrinkage and textured effect of garter stitch are unappealing. In Unst lace, the yarnovers and compensatory decreases are next to each other. Most yarnovers are single, with Bird's Eye (see alternate hexagons, photo, p. 58) forming the largest holes. Only Cat's Eye is habitually worked on a stockinette fabric (see "Shetland lace patterns workshop," p. 60).

In contrast, most established lace patterns are worked on a stockinette ground on fine or medium-weight yarn, with the yarnovers and decreases worked on the right side, and the wrong-side rows purled. This means that each yarnover is worked as a complete stitch on the following row.

Tools and materials—The lace knitters of Unst used the finest handspun wool and fine steel needles, known as "wires," to knit their veils, shawls, and stoles. Wool of this fineness has never been commercially available; it can be produced only by the most highly skilled and patient handspinner. The finest commercially available wool is one-ply Shetland cobweb, in white only. Steel wires are rare today, but sets of five 8-in. double-pointed steel needles can be ordered from the suppliers listed on p. 59. Their sizes range from 00 to 00000. Double-pointed 14-in. steel needles in sizes 0-000 (14-16) can be ordered from Scotland.

Few knitters today have the time or immense patience to knit a very fine lace article. Nevertheless, beautiful knit lace can be made from many modern lightweight yarns with the usual knitting tools. Wool and cotton are the most common and appropriate yarns to use for lace knitting. Wool is easier to control due to its elasticity and is therefore ideal for beginners.

Many knitters wrongly assume that all lace must be knit on fine needles. Needle size should be appropriate for the yarn used so the resulting fabric will have an open appearance. Needles that are too fine for the yarn will produce close-knit fabric without the open quality of lace. Since lace tension will vary from knitter to knitter, it's important to knit experimental swatches to determine the best needle size.

Tension—Even tension is essential to the production of good knit lace, probably more so than with any other type of knitting. Uneven tension will give a ragged, mistake-ridden impression, especially on fine work, where a slightly larger hole here and there will show up all too clearly. The techniques of lace knitting are easy to learn and to execute, but serving an apprenticeship, in which you practice simple lace edgings, such as those in "Knitted-Lace Edgings," *Threads*, No. 18, p. 27, is worthwhile. This is an excellent way to begin mastering an even lace tension, and you can use the edgings as gathered frills to disguise imperfections.

Lace should never be knit with a tight tension, as this will lead to serious difficulty, particularly when you're decreasing several stitches together. Aim for an even, relaxed rhythm. When working with fine yarn, you may find that holding it in your usual way doesn't give you sufficient control. You may need to loop the yarn around your finger one or two more times than usual. Experiment until you find a comfortable method that will give the right amount of control.

Casting on—The usual methods of casting on are too coarse and inelastic to be suitable for lace knitting, especially for very fine and open lace, which has a good deal of lateral stretch. Two types of cast-on, open loop and picot chain (drawings, p. 59), will produce a light, elastic edge.

The open-loop cast-on is especially good when stitches need to be knit up from the cast-on edge. Hold two needles together and make a cast-on slip knot over both with the lace yarn. Cut a length of contrast yarn twice the length to hold all the required stitches and knot it near the tips of the needles. Hold the contrast yarn so that it lies along the needles. Then wind the lace yarn over and around the two needles and contrast yarn in a clockwise direction until the loops and slip knot equal the required number of stitches. Tie the contrast-yarn ends together.

Now pull one needle out, but hold the last loop of the lace yarn in place with one finger. Slip the contrast knot off the needle, and knit one row plain to complete the cast-on edge. The first stitch is difficult. Leave the contrast yarn in place if the cast on edge is to be grafted, or have stitches knit up from it. When you come to that stage, slip a needle through the loops; then untie or cut the contrast yarn and pull it out. Remove the contrast yarn if no further work will be needed at the cast-on edge.

The *picot-chain cast-on* is formed vertically and produces a decorative edge. Distinctive loops at each side make it easy to graft or knit up stitches. Cast on 2 sts. *Bring the yarn forward and slip the 1st st purlwise. Bring the yarn over the needle to the back (forming a picot loop) and knit the 2nd st. Pass the slip stitch over the knit stitch. Be sure to pass the slip stitch over, not the picot loop. Turn the work, and repeat from * until there are as many picot loops along one edge as the required number of stitches, less 1 st. Slip the last picot

Bird's Eye fills alternate hexagons on this detail from the center of an Unst shawl. Single threads on the hexagon outlines and fan shapes result from yarnovers worked on every row.

loop over the stitch on the right needle, leaving 1 st. Then knit up 1 st through each picot loop along one side.

Side selvages—Chain and picot selvages enhance any lace work and make grafting, knitting up stitches, or seaming easy and neat. Remember to cast on enough stitches to work your chosen side selvages.

To work a *chain selvage,* slip the 1st st purlwise, and knit the last stitch on every row. When you knit up stitches from this selvage, each chain, produced by 2 rows, forms the base for 1 st. Work a slightly more complex chain selvage as follows: On the right side, slip the 1st st knitwise, purl the 2nd st; purl the next-to-the-last stitch, and slip the last stitch. On alternate rows, purl the 1st and last 2 sts.

The *picot selvage* complements the picot-chain cast-on. Both are effective where the cast-on and side selvages are plainly visible. To make a picot selvage before a knit stitch (first drawing, bottom left, facing page), bring the yarn to the front, insert the right

needle into the 1st st and knit. A loop forms before the 1st st. Make a single decrease in the next 2 sts, and knit the loop on the return row for best results, or just drop it on the return row.

For a picot selvage before a purl (second drawing, lower left, facing page), take the yarn to the back of the work, insert the right needle into the 1st st and purl. Decrease immediately after the loop, and purl it on the return, or drop it on the return.

Single yarnovers—The yarnover is used to create holes in knit lace. To make a yarnover, throw the yarn around the right needle before putting the needle through the next stitch on the left needle. When worked on the return row, the yarnover becomes a stitch.

Yarnovers vary according to the combination of stitches between which they're made. *Between two knit stitches,* bring the yarn to the front, under the right needle; insert the right needle into the next stitch and knit it. *Between two purl stitches,* take the yarn over and around the right needle; insert

the needle into the next stitch and purl it. *After a knit and before a purl stitch,* bring the yarn to the front, under the right needle, then over and around it. Insert the right needle into the next stitch and purl it. *After a purl and before a knit stitch,* take the yarn over the right needle; insert the needle into the next stitch and knit it.

When the yarnover is worked as one stitch (either knit or purl) on the return row, the resulting hole is called an eyelet, or *single eyelet.* A single yarnover can also be worked as 2 sts on the return row. Notice that this will result in an extra increase. You can (p1, k1), (k1, p1), (p1, p1b—in the back), or (k1, k1b) to produce an open, round form, referred to as a *double eyelet.*

Double yarnovers—If a larger hole is required, throw the yarn around the needle twice before working the next stitch. The double yarnover may occasionally be worked as a single stitch on the return row, although double yarnovers are mainly used for making bold, picot, and grand eyelets, in which 2 sts or more are worked into the two yarnovers on the return row.

To make a *bold eyelet* (used in Bird's Eye), work a double yarnover; then (k1, p1) or (p1, p1b) or (k1, k1b) into the double yarnover on the return row. A *picot eyelet* (Cat's Eye) takes advantage of the fact that working (p1, k1) into a double yarnover produces an effect different from any of the other three methods. The knit stitch will form a small drop in a heart-shaped eyelet. *Grand eyelets* are produced when more than 2 sts are worked into the yarnover(s) on the return row. They range from 3 sts worked into a single yarnover to any number of stitches worked into a multiple one.

Single decreases—Decreases in lace knitting compensate for the extra stitches created by the yarnovers, usually keeping the stitch count constant. Each of the various types of decreases creates a particular effect.

Single decreases, 2 sts reduced to 1 st, will show some slant to the right or left, depending on the method used. Repeated decreases slanting in the same direction will produce a bias fabric like Lace Trellis, shown and described on pp. 60 and 61. Paired decreases, which show the same degree of slant—one decrease to the right and one to the left—will correct bias and produce symmetrical results. Arrowhead Lace (photo, p. 61) is a good example. Both the knit and purl single decreases described below can be worked as symmetrical pairs.

Knit two together (k2tog) slants to the right. Insert the right needle into the front loops of the next 2 sts, putting it through the 2nd st first, and k2tog. The purl-side equivalent is *purl two together* (p2tog). Insert the right needle into the front loops of the next 2 sts, and p2tog.

Slip, slip, knit (SSK) slants to the left. Slip the 1st st and 2nd st, one at a time,

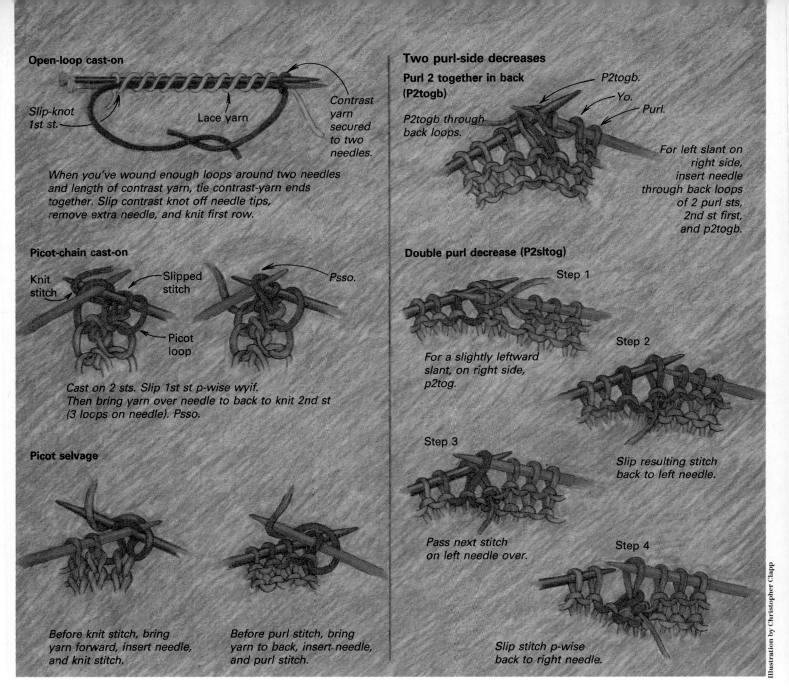

Open-loop cast-on

Slip-knot 1st st.

Lace yarn

Contrast yarn secured to two needles.

When you've wound enough loops around two needles and length of contrast yarn, tie contrast-yarn ends together. Slip contrast knot off needle tips, remove extra needle, and knit first row.

Picot-chain cast-on

Knit stitch

Slipped stitch

Psso.

Picot loop

Cast on 2 sts. Slip 1st st p-wise wyif. Then bring yarn over needle to back to knit 2nd st (3 loops on needle). Psso.

Picot selvage

Before knit stitch, bring yarn forward, insert needle, and knit stitch.

Before purl stitch, bring yarn to back, insert needle, and purl stitch.

Two purl-side decreases

Purl 2 together in back (P2togb)

P2togb.

Yo.

Purl.

P2togb through back loops.

For left slant on right side, insert needle through back loops of 2 purl sts, 2nd st first, and p2togb.

Double purl decrease (P2sltog)

Step 1

For a slightly leftward slant, on right side, p2tog.

Step 2

Slip resulting stitch back to left needle.

Step 3

Pass next stitch on left needle over.

Step 4

Slip stitch p-wise back to right needle.

Illustration by Christopher Clapp

knitwise to the right needle. Then insert the left needle into the front loops of these 2 sts from the left, and knit them together. (For more, see *Threads*, No. 17, p. 38.) On the purl side, *purl two together through the back loops* (p2togb) for the same effect. Insert the right needle into the back loops of the next 2 sts, inserting the needle into the 2nd st first, and p2togb (see drawing at top right).

Multiple decreases—Double decreases reduce 3 sts to 1 st. They can be worked to slant to the right or left or to remain vertical.

Knit three together (k3tog) slants to the right. Insert the right needle into the next 3 sts, starting with the 3rd st, and k3tog. On the purl side, *purl three together* (p3tog).

Slip one knitwise, knit two together, pass the slipped stitch over (sl1-k2tog-psso) slants to the left. *Purl two together, slip stitch to left needle, pass 2nd st on left over, slip stitch to right needle* (p2sltog). The purl-side equivalent (drawings at right, above) slants slightly to the left.

Unst knitters didn't use vertical decreases, but these work well and look nice on some patterns, especially in lace-weight or heavier yarn. On the knit side, *slip 2 sts together knitwise, knit one, pass both slipped stitches over* (sl2tog-k1-p2sso). On the purl side, *Sl2togb-p1-p2sso* produces a vertical effect.

To make more than a double decrease, knit or purl the required number of stitches together. If many stitches are to be decreased together, work them loosely on the previous row. Sometimes it's also helpful to slip the right needle into the decrease stitches to loosen them before you work the decrease. As you knit your way through the workshop on pp. 60-61, you'll find that a loose tension makes decreasing easier.⇨

Alice Starmore is a frequent contributor to Threads. Her book, Alice Starmore's Book of Fair Isle Knitting *(1988), is available from The Taunton Press. Photo on p. 55 courtesy of the Aberdeen University Library; other photos courtesy of the Shetland Museum and Library.*

Supplies

Beggar's Lace
Box 17263
Denver, CO 80217
(303) 722-5557
8-in. steel needles as fine as 00000; 1-ply Shetland cobweb yarn.

Jamieson & Smith
90 North Road
Lerwick, Shetland, Scotland ZEI OPQ
011-44-595-3579
1-ply Shetland cobweb yarn; 2-ply Shetland lace-weight wool (about 20 colors); 14-in. steel needles in sizes 0-000 (14-16).

Patternworks
Box 1690
Poughkeepsie, NY 12601
(914) 454-KNIT
Shetland cobweb and lace-weight yarn; 8-in. steel needles, sizes 00-00000.

Schoolhouse Press
6899 Cary Bluff
Pittsville, WI 54466
(715) 884-2799
Shetland cobweb and lace-weight yarn; 8-in. steel needles, sizes 00-0000.

Shetland lace patterns workshop

There is no doubt that the Unst knitters elevated their lace knitting to an art form. Their mastery of the techniques gave them the freedom to create fantastic, complex patterns, as shown in the photos on pp. 56 and 57. Gaining a complete understanding of the technique and its effects began in childhood with the thoughtful practice of simple patterns. Accordingly, I've planned a series of patterns to assist you in developing the necessary understanding to make even complicated lace patterns easy and fun. Eventually, you may be able to create your own patterns. To gain the most from this "workshop," you must knit a swatch for each pattern in turn, studying what is happening as you knit. Refer to the knitting techniques on pp. 57-59 and the swatches in the photo on the facing page.

Eyelet patterns: Eyelet patterns are the most basic of the lace techniques.

Single Eyelet (multiple of 8 sts) is a stockinette fabric punctuated by single eyelets worked on the right side and spaced at regular intervals. To form the eyelets, work a yo, then a k2tog. The decrease immediately compensates for the new stitch formed by the yo, so the stitch count remains constant throughout.
Row 1 (right side): Knit.
Row 2 and all wrong-side rows: Purl.
Row 3: K6, yo, k2tog; repeat.
Row 5: Knit.
Row 7: K2, *yo, k2tog, k6*, *-* to last 4 sts, end k4.
Row 8: Purl.
Repeat rows 1 through 8.
  Work variations, using an SSK decrease and altering the intervals between eyelets.

Bird's Eye (multiple of 4 sts) is often used to fill geometric shapes in larger designs, such as the diamonds in the detail from a lace stole (p. 56) and alternate hexagons in the detail on p. 58. To form the pattern, work double yo's with compensatory k2tog decreases on each side. Subsequent rows of eyelets are set exactly between the eyelets of the previous row, thus forming a mesh.

Row 1 (wrong side): *K2tog, yo2x, k2tog*; repeat *-*.
Row 2: *K1, (k1, p1) into double yo, k1*; repeat *-*.
Row 3: K2, *k2tog, yo2x, k2tog*; repeat *-* to last 2 sts, k2.
Row 4: K2, *k1, (k1, p) into double yo, K1*; repeat *-* to last 2 sts; k2.
Repeat rows 1 through 4.
  After working this swatch, you're ready to think about how to fill a diamond shape with the pattern. Work the first Bird's Eye on the 4 center sts at the base of the diamond, working rows 1 and 2 of the pattern. To work the two eyelets on the next row, you need 4 more sts—2 sts at each side of the original 4 sts. On these 8 sts, work (k2tog, yo2x, K2tog)2x. Then work row 2 of the pattern over the 8 sts. Continue in this manner, working 2 sts more on each side of the patterned stitches for each new row of eyelets until you've reached the desired width (in the case of the stole, 4 eyelets worked over 16 sts). To taper the pattern to the finish, reverse the procedure. Omit 2 sts on each side of the pattern until the eyelet diamond is complete.
  It's now easy to see how the hexagonal shape in the photo on p. 58 has been filled. The pattern starts with 1 eyelet and increases to 3 eyelets (over 12 sts). It's then worked straight on the 12 sts for 10 rows before it's shaped to completion.

Cat's Eye (multiple of 4 sts) is another Shetland mesh pattern, worked over the same multiple as Bird's Eye, and it can be used in the same way. There are two differences: (p1, k1) is worked into each double yo, thus making a picot eyelet. Also, the decreases are worked on the row following the yo's, so the stitch count varies.

Row 1 (right side): K4, *yo2x, k4*; *-*.
Row 2: P2, *p2tog, (p1, k1) into double yo, p2tog*; *-* to last 2 sts, p2.
Row 3: K2, yo, *k4, yo2x*, *-* to last 6 sts, k4, yo, k2.
Row 4: P3, *p2tog2x, (p1, k1) into double yo*; *-* to last 7 sts, p2tog2x, p3.
Repeat rows 1 through 4.

Faggoting patterns

The patterns so far have displayed a variety of eyelets with compensatory decreases. Innumerable patterns also make use of the single eyelet with various types of decreases to create particular effects. Faggoting, the most basic of all lace patterns, demonstrates this. It is worked by the repeated use of a yo and a single decrease. The two patterns that follow differ only in the type of decrease used; yet the results are very different.

Turkish Faggoting is worked on an even number of sts.
Row 1: K1, *yo k2tog*, *-* to last st; k1.
Repeat this row.

Purse Faggoting (even number of sts).
Row 1: K1, *yo, SSK*; *-* to last st, k1.
Repeat this row.
  Note that because the yo is knit together with another stitch on the following row, it remains as a single thread between the decreases, which can be seen clearly in the fan-shaped patterns in the photo on p. 58. Purling (or knitting) the yo intertwines it with the new stitch and forms two twisted threads, which are more stable than the single thread described above.

Lace Trellis (even number of stitches) is faggoting with a purl row worked on alternate rows. The twisted threads of the yo can be compared with the single thread of faggoting. Because the k2tog decrease slants to the right and is continuously worked on one side only, the fabric has a strong rightward bias.
Row 1 (right side): K1, *yo, k2tog*, *-* to last st, k1.
Row 2: Purl.
Repeat rows 1 and 2.
  To produce a leftward bias:
Row 1 (right side): K1, *SSK, yo*, *-* to last st, k1.
Row 2: Purl.
  Most patterns correct bias by working right and left slanting decreases in equal measure to produce symmetrical patterns. For *Zigzag Lace Trellis,* work the two rightward bias rows several times (e.g., 3 times); then work the two leftward bias rows the same number of times, and repeat. Note that the side selvages will wave to the right and left.

Pictorial patterns: You can form images by locating eyelets strategically.

Arrowhead Lace (multiple of 10 sts + 1 st) is a good example of a simple symmetrical pattern with left- and right-slanting decreases equally balanced on each side of a central vertical double decrease.
Rows 1 and 3 (wrong side): Purl.
Row 2: K1, *(yo, SSK)2x, k1, (k2tog, yo)2x, k1*; *-*.
Row 4: K2, *yo, SSK, yo, sl2tog-k1-p2sso (pass 2 sl sts over), yo, k2tog, yo, k3*, *-* to last 2 sts, k2.
  Make the Arrowhead panels wider by adding 4 more sts to the multiple and working an extra yo, SSK on the right and an extra k2tog, yo on the left. Work a little Arrowhead by omitting 4 sts of the multiple and omitting 1 yo, SSK and 1 k2tog, yo.

Gull's Wings (multiple of 7 sts) is a simple pattern worked as a vertical panel. Though unassuming, it's well worth studying closely. Row 2 is significant in that the right- and left-slanting decreases are placed at each side of a central yo, k1, yo. This forms the opening for a variety of motifs and is an important foundation to keep in mind when you're designing your own lace patterns.
Row 1 (wrong side and all wrong side rows): Purl.
Row 2: K1, k2tog, yo, k1, yo, SSK, k1.
Row 4: K2tog, yo, k3, yo, SSK.
Repeat rows 1 through 4.

Cat's Paw (multiple of 7 sts) is a favorite among the Shetland patterns. Its first 4 rows are Gull's Wings. Row 6 closes the "wings" with a double decrease that is worked over the 3 center sts.
Rows 1-4: Gull's Wings.
Row 5: Purl.
Row 6: K2, yo, sl1-K2tog-psso, yo, k2.
Repeat rows 1 through 6.

Lace Ladders separate the Gull's Wings and Cat's Paws in the photo at right. To form these, work SSK, yo2x, k2tog on the right-side rows. On the reverse, k1, p1 in the double yo.

Shetland Fern (multiple of 15 sts). Instead of opening the motif with two holes at each side of a central stitch, as in the two previous patterns, the Shetland Fern opens with one hole. As a result, the decrease will give a slightly asymmetrical appearance. Symmetry is restored on row 3, where the typical opening row is worked centered over the single hole. The Fern motif can be found in some form or another on practically every piece of Unst lace, where it is usually worked without any purl rows. Here it is worked with a purl wrong side for the first 10 rows; thereafter, yo's and decreases are worked on every row. This makes the left and right decreases curve more steeply toward each other.
Row 1 (right side): K7, yo, SSK, k6.
Rows 2, 4, 6, 8, 10: Purl.
Row 3: K5, k2tog, yo, k1, yo, SSK, k5.
Row 5: K4, k2tog, yo, k3, yo, SSK, k4.
Row 7: K4, yo, SSK, yo, sl1-k2tog-psso, yo, k2tog, yo, k4.
Row 9: K2, k2tog. yo, k1, yo, SSK, k1, k2tog, yo, k1, yo, SSK, k2.
Row 11: K2, (yo, SSK)2x, k3, (k2tog, yo)2x, k2.
Row 12: P3, (yo, p2tog)2x, p1, (p2togb, yo)2x, p3.
Row 13: K4, yo, SSK, yo, sl1-k2tog-psso, yo, k2tog, yo, k4.
Row 14: P5, yo, p2tog, p1, p2togb, yo, p5.
Row 15: K6, yo, sl1-k2tog-psso, yo, k6.
Row 16: Purl.
Repeat rows 1 through 16 for a vertical panel.—A.S.

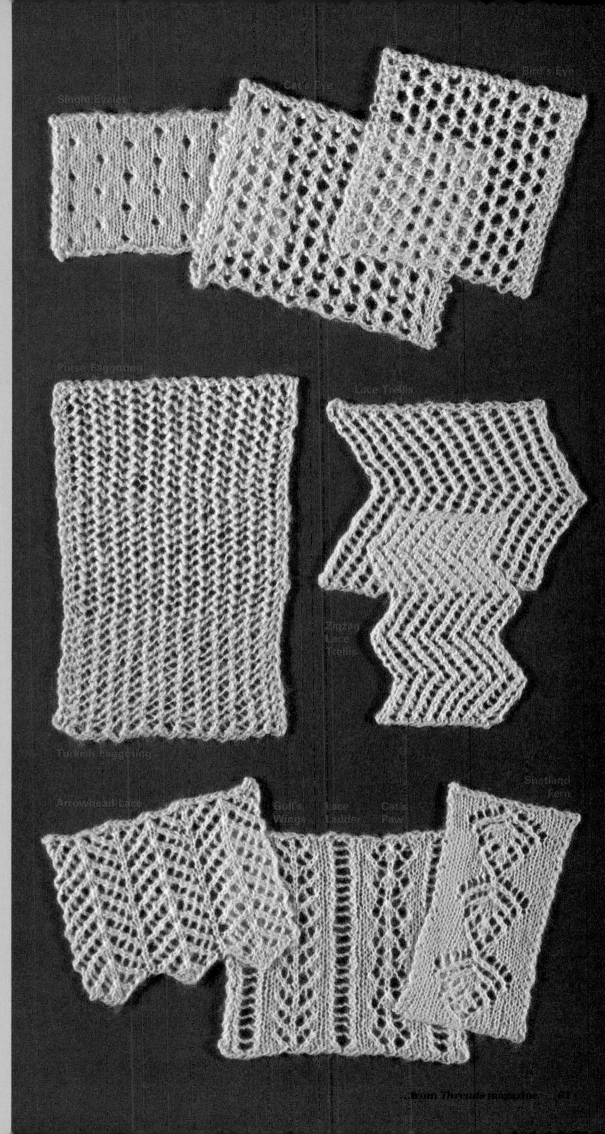

Socks, Socks, Socks

Knit Fair Isles to fit your feet

by Peg Richard

My memories of growing up in Western Maine are filled with the winter smells of wet wool socks drying on radiators. The socks my mother made of thick Canadian wool grew soft and sturdy as they felted with repeated washings. When the heels and toes finally wore out, my mother simply cut the sock off at the bottom of the cuff and knitted the foot again, adding new colors as she grew tired of old.

I began knitting multicolored socks as I became interested in Fair Isle patterns and color theory. Unlike my mother, I put aside sturdy materials for Shetland wools, mohairs, silk, alpaca, and bouclés. Socks are a great size for pattern samples. But since I've become addicted to Fair Isle socks, I've had to take a close look at construction and materials for socks that are both gorgeous and long-wearing.

Choosing yarns

Materials are my first consideration in designing socks. Because Fair Isle designs produce extra thickness, it is important to use fine yarns so the sock will fit inside a shoe, but it must still be strong enough to withstand hard wear. If a yarn pulls apart easily or has a great deal of loft, like the beautifully colored Shetland jumper-weight yarns, it may be too softly spun for the foot of a sock, but fine for the cuff. I prefer multi-plied, tightly spun sports- or fingering-weight yarns, but a well-spun single is also good (see Supplies on p. 65). Some European sock yarns are still available, but difficult to find. Although of fingering weight, they may have as many as four plies, and often come with a small amount of wool and nylon yarn dyed to match for heels and toes. I find that warp yarns are a good alternative.

Some are so finely spun that I may have to combine two or three to achieve the stitch gauge I need, but this is a good way to create new colors. Most weaving suppliers will wind off small amounts of warp yarns.

As a substitute for the nylon blend yarns that used to be readily available for heels and toes, I use fine linen warp yarns. They are thin enough that they can be added to regular yarns at the heels and toes to add long-wearing strength without bulk.

Designing Fair Isle socks

No matter what design I choose, I always knit with Fair Isle methods, using only two colors in any one round and carrying yarn for very small intervals. This produces a dense, warm, durable fabric. I also use needles a size or two smaller than I would for a sweater. Because a densely patterned knit will have less stretch than a plain knit, a patterned gauge swatch is very important.

I often knit a plain foot; but if I carry the pattern onto the foot, I knit the sole in a seeding pattern, as shown on p. 64, right center, so it will be dense and durable. I knit heels and toes without a pattern and often change color to make the stitches easier to pick up for reknitting when they wear out.

Pattern and color

Because a sock has much less design space than a sweater, I choose small patterns with frequent repeats—both horizontally and vertically. I often use a single background color throughout to provide visual unity. These two simple guidelines define the perfect framework for experimentation.

I use color opposites to create vibrant combinations. I will add golds, yellows, and oranges to enliven the coolness of a blue, violet, and purple color family. Reds, pinks, and red-purples brighten with the addition of a little turquoise or jade green. If a color doesn't seem quite right, I often leave it in and keep adding more colors. What first seems like a mistake may actually become an asset.

Planning a straight sock

A boot or crew sock is a perfect project for the beginner. It can be knit in any weight. And because the straight top lacks shaping, colorful designs are easy to plan.

For worsted-weight crew socks you'll need about 4 oz. of a main color, odds and ends of other colors as desired, two sets of four double-pointed needles, sizes 5 and 7, and a blunt-end yarn needle. I generally use the main color for the ribbing, some of the leg pattern, and most of the foot, adding other colors for patterns, heel, and toe. Unless you want unmatched socks, be sure to divide colors in half, one for each sock. Thinner yarns will use fewer ounces, heavier yarns more.

The first step in designing a straight sock is to decide how high it should be. To avoid shaping, choose a height below the widest part of the calf so the sock won't be too wide at the ankle. The other measurements that you will need are the length of the foot and the greatest circumference of the foot (for the sock's circumference).

A pattern that repeats every four, five, or six stitches is a good choice. Peerie patterns from traditional Fair Isle knitting offer endless possibilities (see Books on p. 65). They can be combined and varied with simple stripes to create seemingly more complex patterns.

After knitting a pattern gauge swatch and determining the stitch gauge, multiply the

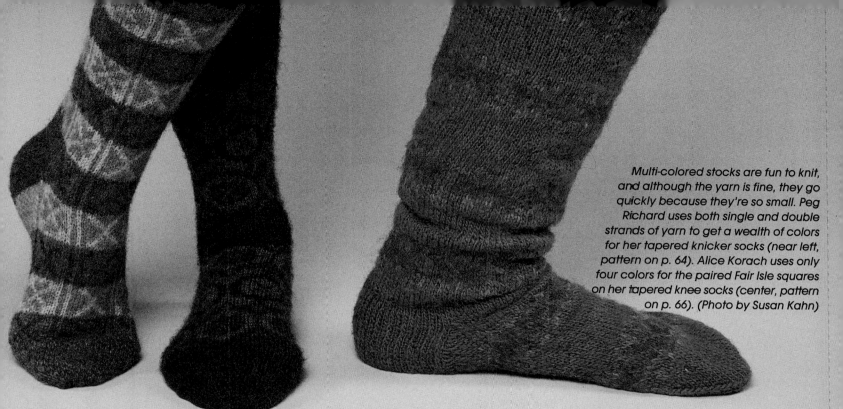

Multi-colored stocks are fun to knit, and although the yarn is fine, they go quickly because they're so small. Peg Richard uses both single and double strands of yarn to get a wealth of colors for her tapered knicker socks (near left, pattern on p. 64). Alice Korach uses only four colors for the paired Fair Isle squares on her tapered knee socks (center, pattern on p. 66). (Photo by Susan Kahn)

number of stitches per inch by the number of inches for the widest part of the sock. If the number of stitches needed doesn't fit your pattern repeat, round it to the closest full pattern.

Knitting a straight sock

Starting at the top of the leg, use the smaller needles to cast on for the rib. Divide onto three needles, join without twisting, and work k1, p1 rib for at least one inch. (See the drawing on p. 64 for all the specific construction details.) Then change to larger needles and begin Fair Isle patterns. I like to weave in the end of each new color as it is added by catching the tail behind every third stitch. If your pattern has long floats, weave them in every few stitches. Carry the yarn with an even, smooth tension.

When the leg is long enough, complete the current pattern, then change to the main color and knit four or six rows. You may want to change back to the smaller needles at this point. They will make a firmer fabric and snugger-fitting foot.

Work the heel back and forth on the center back half of the stitches. Divide the remaining instep stitches on the other two needles. You won't be knitting on them until you've completed the heel. For heels I use a slipstitch pattern that adds little bulk but wears well.

Knit the heel flap until it is as long as it is wide. Then turn the heel, using short rows.

Pick up instep gusset stitches along one side of the heel flap (one stitch every other row). With another needle knit the instep stitches. Then with the third needle pick up the same number of gusset stitches on the

other side of the heel flap, and knit half the heel stitches onto the third needle.

Decrease the gusset stitches every round for heavier yarns and every other round for lighter yarns until you have the same number of stitches as on the round before you began the heel. Continue knitting until the foot is two inches short of the toe.

For the toes, I decrease two stitches on each side of the foot per decrease round until 8-12 stitches remain. Then I break off the yarn, leaving a long tail, and use it to graft the stitches together with Kitchner stitch.

Shaping your socks

Ribbed cuffs for shaped socks, such as kilt hose, knee socks, or knicker socks, which I design heavier than knee socks for cross-country skiing, can be knit in many ways. Kilt hose often sport cabled ribbing; Shetland knitters use corrugated rib, as I did on the sock at right, this page; and Scandinavian designers sometimes include Fair Isle or striped patterns in their ribbings. Whichever method you choose, cast on the same number of stitches for the ribbing as you'll need for the calf. If, however, you're knitting stretchier plain ribbing, start with fewer stitches, increasing to the calf amount before starting the Fair Isle patterns.

The only difference between shaped and straight socks is a few more measurements and some well-placed decreases. In addition to ankle and foot measurements, you'll need the widest circumference of the calf, and length from below the knee to widest part of the calf and from widest part of the calf to the ankle.

After knitting your gauge in pattern, calculate how many sts you need to knit the pat-

tern around the ankle and the widest part of the calf. You'll need to decrease the difference between these two numbers as you knit the lower half of the leg.

Knitting is straightforward. Cast on and knit in ribbing for two to three in. For a foldover cuff, turn the ribbing inside-out before beginning the leg pattern. Knit in pattern until the sock reaches mid-calf. Decrease evenly between mid-calf and ankle, working paired decreases on either side of the stitch that joins the rounds (slip 1, knit 1, pass the slip stitch over—sl 1-k1-psso—or slip two stitches knitwise, one at a time, then knit them together—ssk—before the center stitch and knit 2 together—k2tog—after it). Work the heel and foot as you would for a straight sock.

Knitting knicker socks

Knit a pair of shaped socks with this pattern for knicker socks or knee socks.

Needles: Four size 3 double-pointed needles, 7-8 in. length. Blunt tapestry needle.

Yarn: Four oz. sport-weight plum (MC), one oz. each gold, medium gold, orange, royal blue, and jade green. I used Brown Sheep Company single-ply sport-weight yarn and Christopher Farm single-ply yarn. (See Supplies on p. 65.) The medium-gold and orange yarns are fine weaving yarns, color blended by working two strands together.

Gauge and size: 7 sts and 7½ rows = 1 in. Size is medium.

Knitting directions: With MC, cast on 84 sts and divide on three ndls. Work one rnd k1, p1 rib. Then work k1, p1 corrugated rib in main color and orange shading to gold for 1½ in. Knit MC for four rnds. Begin patt, as shown on chart at upper right, p. 64. Work until 6½

Sock-knitting steps

(See pp. 63 and 66 for specific patterns.)

1. Knit a sock in the round (on 4 needles) from the ribbing down, tapering the leg as needed along the center back.

2. At the top of the heel, put the center back half of the sts on one needle, and knit the heel flap back and forth.

3. Continuing with 2 needles, turn the heel by working short rows outward from the central sts on the flap.

4. Pick up sts along the selvedges of the flap, and knit the foot around on the heel, selvedge, and instep sts (4 needles).

5. Decrease alongside the instep to shape the instep gusset.

6. When the foot is long enough, decrease toe.

7. Graft the last 2 in. of sts together.

Gusset decrease:

Decrease on the three sts next to the instep, as you knit around the foot, until same number of sts as at the ankle remain. With heavier yarns, decrease every round; with fingering or light sport yarns, decrease every other round as foll: On 3 sts before instep: Sl 1-k1-psso or ssk, k1; on 3 sts after instep: k1, k2tog.

Toe decrease:

For a long toe, decrease over the last 2 in.—4 sts on each decrease round—every round for heavier yarn; every other round for lighter yarn, as foll: On the last 3 sts of the sole and instep, sl 1-k1-psso or ssk, k1; on the first 3 sts of the instep and sole, k1, k2tog. For a shorter toe, plan any number of decreases (k2tog) evenly spaced around the toe for the number of rounds desired.

Grafting

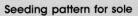

Illustrations by Mary Bressler

Use Kitchner st to join the sole and instep at the toe-tip. Leave last 2 to 3 in. of toe sts undecreased—1 to 1½ in. each on instep and sole. Graft instep sts to sole sts with yarn tail, and weave end in.

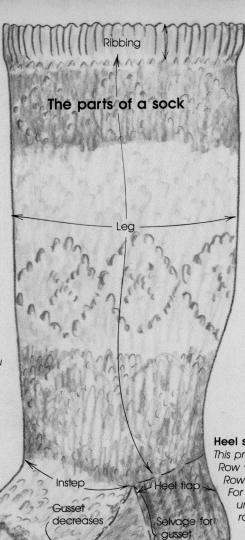

The parts of a sock

Ribbing

Leg

Instep

Gusset decreases

Instep gusset

Heel flap

Selvage for gusset pick-up

Heel turn

Sole

Toe decreases 2 in.

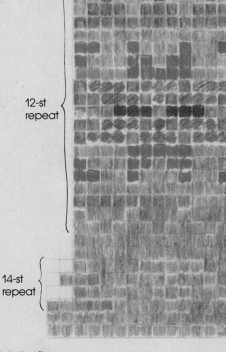

Peg Richard's knicker sock chart

12-st repeat

14-st repeat

Heel stitch for flap:

This produces a long-wearing heel:
Row 1 (RS): *Sl 1, k1*, repeat *-* to end.
Row 2 (WS): Purl.
For a deep heel counter work these two rows until flap is as long as it is wide; or work as many rows as stitches for a shallower counter.

Seeding pattern for sole

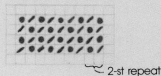

2-st repeat

Round heel:

With the center stitch clearly marked, turning a heel with short rows is easy.
Row 1 (RS): On knit side, k to 2 sts past center st, *sl 1-k1-psso, k1, turn.*
Row 2 (WS): Sl 1, purl to 3 sts past center st, *p2tog, p1, turn.*
Row 3: Sl 1, k to 3 sts past center st, work *-* row 1.
Row 4: Sl 1, p to 4 sts past center st, work *-* row 2.
Repeat in this manner, each time knitting or purling 1 more st and then decreasing, until all sts have been worked. See the chart below for a schematic presentation of the process.

Turning a round heel

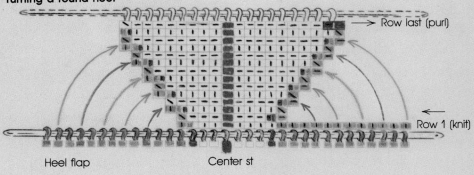

Row last (purl)

Row 1 (knit)

Heel flap   Center st

Key to symbols   ┃ Knit   – Purl   ╲ Slip   ▦ Sl 1-k1-psso   ╌ P2tog

This chart is based on one that appears in Mary Thomas's Knitting Book (New York: Dover Publications, Inc., 1971).

in. from beg, or desired length to widest part of calf. Continuing in patt, dec 2 sts every 4th rnd, six times as foll: at beg of rnd, k2tog; work in pattern to last 3 sts of rnd and sl 1-k1-psso or ssk; k1 (last st of rnd)—72 sts. Continue in patt until sock measures 15½ in., or desired length to ankle.

Place 36 sts on one ndl for heel; center st is last st of rnd. Follow directions for heel stitch at center right, facing page, working in MC.

When heel is done, pick up sts for gussets and work as described at far left until 72 sts remain. Work foot using a seeding patt, as shown at left for the sole and the Fair Isle patt on top. When 2 in. from end of foot, dec for toe, as described at far left center, facing page, using MC only. Graft last 6 toe sts tog.

The long-lived sock

To keep my socks long-lasting I wash them often and give them a rest between wearings. When the heels and toes wear out, I either cut the sock off at the foot and reknit the whole foot or reknit the worn out part. You can reknit a turned heel this way: Cut off the old heel and unravel the yarn until a clear line of stitches is visible. Pick up the heel stitches at the top of the heel. Don't unravel beyond the instep gusset. Work the heel back and forth, picking up stitches on the sides of the heel as you knit to join the new heel to the foot as you go. When the heel flap is long enough, turn the heel normally, leaving the same number of stitches on the heel as on the sole. Graft them together with Kitchner stitch.   ⇨

Peg Richard is a textile artist, art educator, and addicted Fair Isle knitter who lives in Portland, Maine.

Books

Duncan, Ida Riley. *The Complete Book of Progressive Knitting.* New York: Liveright, 1968 (orig. pub 1940).

MacGregor, Sheila. *The Complete Book of Traditional Fair Isle Knitting.* New York: Charles Scribner's Sons, 1981.

Starmore, Alice. *Alice Starmore's Book of Fair Isle Knitting.* Newtown, CT: The Taunton Press, 1988.

Supplies

Brown Sheep Co., Inc.
Route 1
Mitchell, NE 69357
(308) 635-2198
Call or write for local distributor

Christopher Farm Yarns
RFD #1, Box 1373
Richmond, ME 04357
(207) 666-5942
Swatch card

Patternworks
Box 1690
Poughkeepsie, NY 12601
(914) 462-8000
Polyester heel and toe filament, fine linen yarns

Tomato Factory Yarn Co.
8 Church St.
Lambertville, NJ 08530
(609) 397-3475
Shetland yarns

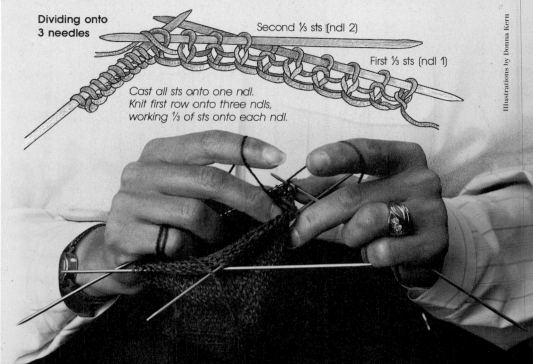

Dividing onto 3 needles

Second ⅓ sts (ndl 2)

First ⅓ sts (ndl 1)

Cast all sts onto one ndl. Knit first row onto three ndls, working ⅓ of sts onto each ndl.

Illustrations by Donna Kern

Starting on four double-pointed needles

At first, everyone feels awkward knitting on four double-pointed needles. But with practice, you learn to control all those extra points. Here are some of my tricks.

Your stitches will form a triangle with approximately one-third of the stitches on each needle. The fourth needle is for knitting. It's easiest to knit on double-pointeds if the stitches are evenly distributed because the work is balanced. Pick needles that will be three to five inches longer than the longest span of stitches that each must hold. Needles that are too long unbalance the stitches and twist them out of position. But if the needles are too short, stitches will slip off the ends.

Cast on onto a single needle, and divide the stitches as you knit the first row: After knitting one-third of the stitches, pick up another needle and knit the next third onto it, and so forth. To join the round, don't turn the work over. Hold the needle with the last-knit stitches (N3) in your right hand and hold the empty needle in your right hand in front and almost parallel to it. Pick up the needle with the first-knit stitches (N1) in your left hand, and bring it around to insert the empty needle (knitting ndl) into the first stitch. Snug the yarn up and knit it—*but only after you're absolutely sure that the cast-on edge is at the bottom on all the needles and that the stitches haven't twisted around a needle.* If you join the work with a twist, you will produce a moebius strip, and the only solution is to rip. Everyone does it—once.

Many people complain of gaps or tight areas at the change-of-needle points. You can prevent these related problems by holding the knitting needle very close to N3 when you start on a new needle, inserting it into the first stitch from under (in front of) N3. To prevent excessive tightness, be sure the stitches on N3 are spread naturally, and that the new stitches don't bunch up. The left end of every needle in the triangle should be on top of the next needle to make knitting around easy. Otherwise working will become difficult as you approach a needle's end and your tension will change, making the fabric uneven.

There are many ways to hold the needles as you knit, but here's how I do it. I try to keep the stitches on ndls 2 and 3 centered, and I support the end of the knitting needle against my body at about my waist. Mostly I just stick it into the sweater I'm wearing. If you're knitting Continental-style with one color, you can just hold it in your right hand.

I hold the two needles I'm working with gently between my thumbs and middle fingers. As I knit up the stitches on N1, the point of N2 works toward my thumb joint and that of N3 works back toward the base of my thumb until it may go under the palm of my hand and finally out behind, **(photo above)**. When N3 is under my palm, the stitches may tend to slide off the point, so I keep an eye on it, readjusting it as necessary.

The key to getting comfortable with double-pointed needles is to hold the working needles gently and to support the knitting needle. As long as your work isn't too loose, the other needles will take care of themselves.   —Alice Korach

Socks that fit

by Alice Korach

When you buy knee socks that fit well, giving some support and staying up, they're always smaller around than your leg. So when I decided to replace my worn out socks with handknitted Fair Isle socks, I wondered how much smaller to plan them. Nobody seemed to have explored this issue. The closest I came was a ribbed sock pattern with a stockinette stitch gauge and intended leg measurements. The cast-on was about 60-67% of the size of the leg. Requiring a sock to stretch that much is fine with stretchy fabric. In fact, it will fit perfectly at the ankle and foot with no shaping. But stranded knitting is another ball game; it has very little stretch.

The first sock I made was based on a favorite old ski sock that was about 8 in. around. When I'd knit about 5 in., the sock looked too narrow, so I put the stitches on a thread and tried to shove the tube up my leg. It made a great tourniquet.

My next attempt was almost 2 in. bigger around. It looked good so I kept going all the way to the toe, with a minor ripping digression at the heel flap. Mary Thomas says you knit back and forth on the flap until you have a square piece. This resulted in too deep a heel counter. I found that just short of a square fits me well. This sock fit the wide part of my calf fine and stayed up, but it was too loose at my ankle, and the foot was a bit baggy.

Sock number three, shown on p. 63 at left, solved all the problems. I put on my baggy sock, pinched it where my calf started to narrow, counted the number of stitches I pinched out at the ankle so it would fit close but not tight, and calculated the taper evenly in the 44 remaining rows to the start of the heel.

Now I design all my Fair Isle socks 70-80% of my calf circumference with a taper to fit my ankle circumference

snugly. I find that 100% of the actual ankle circumference in stitches, plus or minus a bit, gives a nice-fitting foot. For a yarn that will shrink slightly (all wool), taper to 100%; for a nylon/wool blend, 95% of the true ankle might fit better.

To calculate how many stitches to decrease over what length for the taper, I measure from about an inch below the middle of my calf to my ankle. Then I measure the circumference of my ankle, calculate how many stitches that is in my gauge, and subtract

that number from the number of calf stitches to get the number of stitches to decrease. Since I decrease two stitches per round, there are half as many decrease rounds as decreases; I divide the number of rounds remaining to the ankle by the number of decrease rounds to figure out what the frequency is.

Instructions

Yarn requirements: Four colors of Shetland jumper-weight yarn: two oz. each of two dark colors (used for heels and toes), and one oz. each of two light colors. I used hot pink and dark green for one

band and pink and light green for the other.

Needles: Four double-pointed 7- or 8-in. long size 2 ndls, or size needed for gauge.

Gauge: 8 sts and 9½ rows = 1 in. Note: If you prefer a tighter rib, knit with needles 1 or 2 sizes smaller.

Knitting directions: This sock is 14¾ in. long to top of heel. To lengthen or shorten the leg, make more or fewer pattern bands. For a knee sock, the rule of thumb is to make the leg twice the length

of the foot, not counting ribbing. **Rib:** Cast on 76 sts and work k2, p2 rib as foll: 6 rnds hot pink, 3 rnds pink, 2 rnds dark green, 3 rnds pink, 6 rnds hot pink. **Leg:** Work first row of pattern on chart at center, increasing 2 sts—78. There are 26 sts per ndl. Work 7 patt bands, or desired number to 1 in. past mid-calf. **Begin taper:** Note that center back st is center st of second patt on needle 1. Starting with row 1 of next band, dec 1 st each side of center back st every 8th rnd, 5 times. Work dec as foll: Work to 2 sts before center back st, sl 1-k1-psso, k center st, k2tog; complete rnd. Keep to patt. On 8th rnd after last dec,

work vertical double dec as foll: work to 1 st before center back st. Slip 2 sts tog kwise-k1-pass 2sl sts over—66 sts. Complete patt band.

Heel: Reposition sts on needles with ½ on N1 (33 sts), and ¼ each on N2 and N3. Center st on N1 is vertical double dec st at center back of leg. (Don't work sts on N3 in last rnd that must be moved to N1.) Alternate 2 rows with one dark color, then 2 rows with the other, working heel stitch as described on p. 64 for the same number of rows as sts, plus 1 to end with WS row—34 rows.

Turn heel: Continue working with same pair of colors alternating 1 st in each as shown in seeding patt, p. 64, to turn heel as described on p. 64. End with purl row—19 sts.

Instep gusset: Change to other pair of colors. N1: Knit across heel in seeding patt. Pick up and knit ½ the number of sts as rows in heel flap along side of heel—17 sts. N2: Pick up 2 sts in corner of sole and instep, working them in background color of patt block. Work across all instep sts in patt. Pick up 2 corner sts to complete third patt block. N3: Pick up 17 sts on side of heel flap working in seeding patt. Knit 9 heel sts. Rnd now begins in center of sole—90 sts.

Decrease gusset: Dec 24 sts, 12 on each side of instep, 1 pair every other rnd, to reestablish 66 sts on foot. Work dec rnds as foll: Last 3 sts N1: Sl 1-k1-psso, k1; first 3 sts N3: k1, k2tog. Keep k1 sts adjacent to instep in green to frame pattern.

Foot: Work even as est until 2 in. before desired length.

Toe: Dec every other rnd as described on p. 64, working in seeding patt and dark colors around. When 22 sts remain, put sts on N1 and N3 on one ndl, and graft to 11 sts on N2.

Finishing: Weave in ends. Make second sock to match. Hand wash socks and dry flat. To increase their durability, make the feet a little long and felt socks lightly, washing and drying once on gentle cycle. □

Alice Korach is an associate editor of Threads.

Fair Isle pattern chart for leg and instep

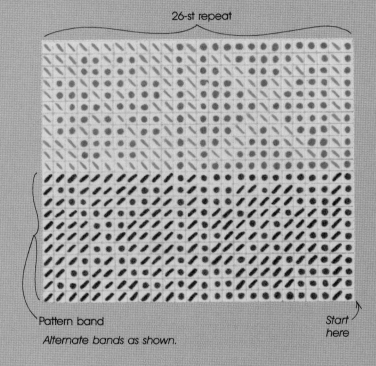

26-st repeat

Pattern band

Alternate bands as shown.

Start here

Catalán Knit Lace

German daily patterns in Spanish hands

by Montse Stanley

One of the most vivid memories of my childhood in Barcelona is of helping to stretch knit lace mats. The mats were washed, dried, dipped into hot starch, and then stretched on a wooden board, into which brass nails had been hammered to conform to each mat's outline. Our mats were mainly circular, with many crochet loops around the edge—hundreds sometimes. The loops made an ideal finish for the edge. Not only did they look good, but because each of the loops could be secured with a nail, they were ideal for stretching the mat. The almost unavoidable center hole was another feature put to good use. A nail driven through it, at the start of the process, ensured even stretching in all directions.

After lifting the knitting from the hot starch mixture, only those with well-seasoned hands could hook many loops without blowing on their fingers. But we couldn't wait for it to cool because it might start to dry before it was fully in position. If the mat was very large, every available pair of hands would be called to the task. The hardest part came at the end when the hot, wet, reluctant mat had to be hooked over the last few nails. Then it was left flat or upright to dry.

To free the mat from the board we pulled the nails with a pair of pliers, taking great care not to touch the knitting. When half the nails had been removed, the mat could be lifted and, if it was not perfectly smooth, pressed on the wrong side with a hot iron.

In the mid-1950s, the craze for lace knitting started to fade. The slow end to Spain's isolation after the civil war, plus an equally slow liberalization of women's lives, inevitably brought deep changes in attitude. Now few knitters are left with the time or patience required to knit a mat, although many still hang on to old favorites, and younger generations are discovering discarded treasures in antique shops.

Sometimes I stretch a few mats for an exhibition. To stretch mats nowadays, I simplify the procedure, pinning the clean, dry mat on a foam mattress, using 2-in.-long glass-headed pins, and then dampen-

When Stanley saw a picture of a new Viennese mat that was nearly identical to this one, which had been in her family's Barcelona home for 50 years, she began her quest for the origin of the design, finally tracing it to Germany. (Photo by Susan Kahn)

Knitters favored circular mats. They divide evenly into a wide variety of geometric shapes and fit comfortably on four or six double-pointed needles. (Photo by Montse Stanley)

Knitters often joined small mats (above) by crocheting their edge loops together. After joining this patchwork, the knitter picked up stitches for a knit border, then finished off with more crochet loops. (Photo by Montse Stanley)

To avoid a gap when changing needles (below), Stanley advises holding the new needle over the old one while pushing the knitting away with the left thumb.

ing the mat with spray starch or plain water. The greatest difficulty is to get the right shape. I draw several concentric circles with a waterproof pen on an old cloth and secure the edges of the cloth to the mattress. I then choose two circles that give the correct outline for the peaks around the edge and for the hollows. If I'm not certain of the final size, pinning the tip of the peaks and the bottom of the hollows is often sufficient to check whether a certain pair of circles gives the right stretch. Of course, symmetrical points need to be equally spaced, so before pinning, I draw radial lines to divide the circle into as many identical segments as required.

Knitting mats

If so much effort and ingenuity went into looking after knit mats, even more went into designing and making them. Mostly, mats were worked from the center out, in a spiral of rows, increasing all the time. The pattern emerged from a combination of lace stitches and increases. Geometric patterns, like the pinwheel and many starlike arrangements such as the one on the mat in the photo above, have a clear structure. They make a good introduction to lace knitting because they are easy to understand and to follow. Free-form patterns are much more intricate. The increases are hidden within the design, not in perfectly arranged lines, so mistakes are easier to make.

Tools and materials—The majority of the mats I've seen have been worked in white or ecru crochet cotton. Occasionally, I've come across colored ones made in artificial silk. Thickness is a personal choice, depending on the size and effect required. Generally, the finer the cotton, the smaller, but more beautiful, the results. However, very fine threads require great confidence. Nowadays, instructions often recommend No. 20 cotton. In old patterns from Barcelona I've found nothing thicker than No. 40. Araceli Miró, a woolshop assistant since the 1940s, says that Nos. 70, 80, and 100 were popular in her early days.

Such fine cotton requires equally fine steel needles, well under 1 mm sometimes. Thick needles give a very open mesh and an unclear pattern. Fine needles make the solid areas compact so they stand out from the lines of holes. The finest needles I've traced in Europe are Inox's 1.25 mm. They come in sets of five, in 8 and 12 in. lengths. This corresponds to an old English size 17 (American 0000). Much finer ones were manufactured in the past. The finest notch in a brass gauge registered some 150 years ago is for size 28. Fine needles are made of steel wire. If you can ask a friend who's good at metalwork to cut the wire to size and taper the ends to a smooth point, you are in business.

In addition to a crochet hook and one or more sets of double-pointed needles, Catalans used several gadgets for knitting lace mats. Sheaths were an invaluable aid for working with double-pointed needles. A Catalan knitter always anchors the right needle by tucking it under the arm or occasionally resting it on the forearm. This requires needles at least 14 in. (35 cm) long—much longer than those used for lace mats, hence the sheath. Catalan sheaths look rather like cigarette holders, except that the hole doesn't go all the way through. They can be fixed at the waist with a cord or ribbon, or tucked into a belt. The free end of a double-pointed needle is then inserted into the sheath, which gives the needle the desired support and leaves the right hand free to move and feed the yarn.

Stitch stops or needle guards, a pair of wooden hoods on opposite ends of a piece of elastic, were used then as now to protect the points of the needles and to prevent crowded stitches from dropping when the work was put aside.

Circular mats—The most popular shape for a mat was circular, with the number of edge peaks depending on the increase arrangement. With rare exceptions, a knitter started the mats at the center, either by casting on 1 st or 2 sts on several double-pointed needles or by using a *pinhole* cast-on. Several crochet slip stitches were worked around a loop of yarn and placed on the knitting needles (instead of being left on the hook to be closed by the next stitch). When the knitting was finished, the original loop was drawn closed and the end darned in. Common cast-on amounts were a total of 6 sts over three needles for mats with six or 12 sections, and 8 sts over four needles for mats with eight or 16 sections. This kept the work neatly divided, but it was easier to check progress with the second arrangement because a circle fits better within a square than within a triangle. So in the case of six or 12 sections, the number of needles might be increased to six after a few rounds.

An extra needle was used to start the first round over the stitches of the first needle, increasing as required. When the first needle was free, it was used to continue the round over the stitches of the second needle, and so on. The knitter took great care to avoid gaps when changing needles. I don't know whether Catalan knitters had a special trick, but a good way of avoiding gaps is to keep the free needle (which has just moved to the right hand) on top of and nearly parallel to the one holding the stitches last made, as shown in the lower photo, facing page. When the work overgrew the original needles, one had three options: add more needles, get longer needles, or change to a circular needle completely made of steel.

Noncircular mats—Shapes other than circles also were popular. For example, a knitter could change a circle into an oval by working two wings, to and fro, over two opposing groups of stitches, while the remaining stitches were left in waiting (see the mat on page 67). Having achieved the desired shape, the knitter worked a more or less deep border over the stitches left in waiting plus new stitches picked up around the side wings. To produce a square instead of a circle, one kept the increases to the change-of-needle lines, having distributed the stitches over four needles. The increase lines formed the square's diagonals. To make a rectangle, one used a *center-*

line cast-on: Twice the number of stitches required for the centerline were cast on by an ordinary method, either on a set of double-pointed needles or on a circular needle, leaving a longish yarn end. The cast-on circle was closed, and the work continued in rounds, concentrating the increases on two pairs of lines—one emanating from the start and the other from the midpoint of the cast-on circle. When the work was completed, the knitter spread it flat and slip-stitched the two sides of the cast-on together with the yarn end.

Finishing mats—Casting off was done with loops of crochet chains, or *long chain cast-off*: The last knit stitch was transferred to a hook; a chain long enough to make a loop was worked; several stitches were then caught with the hook; and a single-crochet stitch was made over these to attach the chain (drawing on page 71). Knitters sometimes added extra rounds of staggered chain loops, each new loop being joined to the center stitch of a loop from the previous round. A similar technique was used to make patchwork arrangements. One small mat was made and cast off with long loops; as the neighboring mats were cast off, the center stitches of their loops were joined to the center stitches of loops on adjacent mats (upper right photo, facing page). The whole could then be finished with extra rounds of loops or with a knit border worked from stitches picked up from

This fine mat requires about 500 pins for stretching. Since some of the sections don't match, and there are varying numbers of leaves on the outer circles, Stanley speculates that it was made by a careless or elderly knitter. (Photo by Montse Stanley)

the edge loops with the same crochet technique used in pinhole cast-on. The border was finally cast off with more chain loops.

The origin of Catalan lace mats
One of my greatest knitting surprises was seeing an oval "Viennese lace" mat on p. 8 of Tessa Lorant's *Hand and Machine Knitted Laces* (Batsford, 1982; out of stock). Except for two narrow bands of stocking stitch, which were missing, it was exactly like the inside of a mat my sister-in-law "had always seen at home," just outside Barcelona! The Catalan mat, now in my possession and shown on page 67, was probably made in the 1930s. Tessa Lorant had bought hers, brand new, in 1981, in a Viennese shop that employed a few outworkers in their sixties or older. Clearly, the pattern was too complex to have been created by two designers from such different backgrounds. I set out to find the link, only to come across another surprise.

The Bishop of Leicester, who was then putting the finishing touches to *A History of Handknitting* (Batsford, 1987; distributed by Interweave Press), told me that while researching his book he had been told by museums in Vienna that there was no such thing as Viennese knit lace. Further

Knit a handkerchief with miniature leaf edging

The finer the thread and fabric, the more delicate this handkerchief edged with miniature leaf lace will be.

This lace pattern is easily adjustable because of its very short pattern repeat (6 sts). It can be used for edging a handkerchief, or for any other situation in which a lace edging is required.

You'll need cotton lawn, knitting yarn, a crochet hook, and a set of five double-pointed needles. The hook must be able to go through the cloth after one thread has been pulled without damaging it. Suitable fine yarns include crochet cotton, lacemaking thread, or even sewing cotton or linen. Size 30 crochet cotton (Daisy by Lily or Big Ball by Coats & Clark) works well with size 000 or 0000 knitting needles and a size 12 or 13 steel crochet hook. The original handkerchief (photo at left) is worked with thread finer than standard tatting cotton.

Swatching—Following the repeat highlighted in green in the chart, knit a sample that's 24 sts x 24 rows (4 repeats x 3 repeats), purling the plain rows. Be careful to align the stitches as shown on the chart. The edges will be tricky on this flat swatch; work single decreases or knit them plain, as required, to maintain the pattern. If your sample feels either stiff or floppy, try again with different needles until it feels nicely firm but supple. Stretch and pin it down, spray it with cold water, and let it dry.

Preparing the cloth—Wash or soak the cloth overnight to preshrink it. Then dry and iron it. To make the handkerchief pull four threads to outline a square approximately 5¼ in. (13.4 cm) on a side, as shown in the drawing at right. Pull the threads by lifting a tail near the edge with a pin; then pull gently with one hand while gathering the cloth with the other. If the thread breaks, pull the end in your hand free and lift a new tail of the same thread. Pull a second set of four threads approximately ¼ in. outside the first square, just far enough for a narrow (⅛-in.) single-fold hem. The sides of the hemmed outer square in the original handkerchief measure just over 5½ in. (14 cm). Cut the cloth carefully along the outer pulled line.

Fold the hem and work a row of single crochet around the edge, inserting the hook into the line of pulled threads (drawing at right). Keep the stitches fairly loose and close, but uncrowded. Depending on your cloth, you'll probably need to skip two to four threads between stitches. Try to work the same number of stitches on each side plus 1 extra st at each corner to square it.

Knitting the edging—From your swatch, calculate the exact width of one pattern repeat. The original measures

---

enquiries had revealed that the expression, often used in Britain, had been coined by Marianne Kinzel, the author of the *First Book of Modern Lace Knitting* (1954) and the *Second Book of Modern Lace Knitting* (1961, both reprinted by Dover). A frail old lady when the Bishop contacted her, she told him how she had first used the words, never thinking that she was coining an expression that other knitters would take literally to describe a kind of knitting unknown in Britain but popular in her native Vienna.

The mystery finally started to unravel in January of 1987. On a visit to Barcelona, I persuaded my mother to ask some of her friends to search for their old pattern books. Two of them produced the original instructions for my version of the oval mat. It was neither Spanish nor Austrian. It was German and had appeared in *Kunst-stricken*, a pattern book (No. 288) published by Otto Beyer. I've been unable to find a date in any copies of the book traced so far. A talk with one of my mother's friends and photographs of people in the books suggest the 1930s.

The attraction of the Beyer books lay in the loose, huge sheets of beautifully clear charts that came with them. A knitter with moderate experience needed no more than a key to symbols, much like the one that accompanies the chart on the facing page, to follow the most intricate designs.

My mother's friends also showed me Spanish pattern books. None of the ones I've seen so far quite matches the quality of the Beyer designs, but this is not surprising. Beyer employed an exceptional designer, Herbert Niebling, who had the extraordinary talent of being able to chart a mat without first sketching it. Some of his

themes are staggering: Oak branches, ferns, or lilies of the valley flow free and fresh, as if they were not constrained by strict counts of increases, decreases, and overs. The Beyer archives were eventually acquired by *Anna Burda*, where nowadays Niebling designs appear, some for the first time. I am certain that some of the mats I have found in Barcelona are copies of his designs. Others are too, I suspect.

Adaptations of mat patterns

Shoulder capes are among the most obvious adaptations of a mat pattern. Typical granny garments, they were worn at home to keep the body warm but the forearms free from bulky sleeves. To make a cape out of a mat, use thicker needles and wool instead of fine cotton. Start the pattern some way up, rather than in the center, to make room for the neck. You work back and

13.8 mm per repeat, about $^9\!/_{16}$ in. Work out how many repeats are needed along each side, rounding up to a full number, if necessary. Then "knit up" 5 sts from under the crochet chains for each repeat required, or use the crochet hook to pull up the stitches and place them on the knitting needles. Space the stitches as evenly as possible, missing chains as necessary, and knit up 1 extra st right on each corner. Use one knitting needle for each side, with a corner stitch at the end of each needle. Work from the chart (always reading from right to left), and add as many eight-row repeats as desired. The original has two. Knit the corner stitches in the back loop for a crisp effect. To avoid gaps when changing needles, always place the new, empty needle on top of the one you've just filled with stitches (see photo, page 68, lower right).

Casting off and finishing—Cluster the stitches in alternate groups of 5 sts and 3 sts, following the chart and the illustrations for long chain cast-off at far right. Work 7 chains between groups. Darn in and trim yarn ends. Stretch and pin down each chain loop, using rustproof pins. Spray the handkerchief with water or aerosol starch, and let it dry flat. Unpin, and press the cloth if necessary. —M.S.

Miniature leaf edging pattern

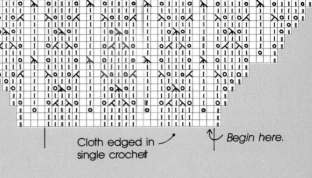

Key to symbols

▫ *Knit.*

▫ *Yarn over.*

▫ *K2tog (knit 2 together).*

▫ *SSK (slip 2 knitwise, knit together).*

▫ *Slip 1, k2tog, pass slip stitch over.*

⌒ *Crochet cast-off together.*

▫ *Space left for stitches to be added (ignore for all practical purposes).*

Cloth edged in single crochet

Begin here.

Corner stitch (in red, knit in back loop)
Pattern repeat (in green, 6 sts x 8 rows)

Preparing the cloth

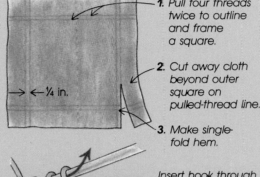

1. Pull four threads twice to outline and frame a square.

2. Cut away cloth beyond outer square on pulled-thread line.

3. Make single-fold hem.

Insert hook through pulled thread line from front of cloth. Draw through a loop. Yarn over and draw another loop through two loops on hook. Repeat around.

Single-fold hem

Pulled thread line

Long chain cast-off

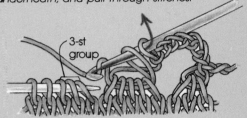

7-chain loop

5-st group

Make 7 chain sts. Insert hook through 5 sts on knitting needle. Catch yarn from underneath, and pull through stitches.

3-st group

Yarn over and pull through two loops on hook. Alternate pulling yarn through 5 sts, then 3 sts, with 7-chain loop between each group.

Illustration by Phoebe Gaughan

forth instead of in rounds to leave a front opening. If the fullness of a circle isn't wanted, one or more repeats can easily be omitted. Catalan knitters usually gave the front edges some sort of knit-in border, or edged them with crochet. The neckline would sometimes be worked in a solid pattern, such as garter stitch, and turned into a hem to make a casing for a ribbon.

Lace-edged handkerchiefs, knit or otherwise, were extremely popular. Catalan knitters showed great ingenuity in joining the knitting and cloth without any sewing. See the directions above for making a handkerchief. After edging the cloth with a crocheted border, you pick up stitches on four double-pointed needles and work a section from a mat chart.

Increases are restricted to the corners and are often the highlight of the design. If a part with suitable increases isn't available, choose a strip without increases and place a mirror on it at a 45° angle to work out the corner. I've seen this kind of mitered corner, worked from the cloth out, in central European publications, but never in British work. Instead, there are a number of Edwardian patterns for edgings worked sideways, where corners are turned with greater or lesser inspiration. I've never seen these in Spain.

It looks as if someone ought to go further into national differences in lace knitting, or into the development of lace knitting in general, which some believe was first worked on a machine. Now there's a subject!

Montse Stanley, now living in Cambridge, England, is the author of several books on knitting design and technique, most recently, Knitting Plus *(1989, B.T. Batsford, Ltd, London).*

Sources

Anna: Burda Knitting & Needlecrafts German Language Publications (distributor)
560 Sylvan Ave.
Englewood Cliffs, NJ 07632
This monthly magazine frequently features knit lace designs, including some Niebling masterpieces; U.S. edition $36 per year.

Beggars' Lace
Box 17263
Denver, CO 80217
(303) 722-5557
8-in. double-pointed needles in sets of 5, sizes 0-00000; lacemaking threads.

Lacis
2982 Adeline St.
Berkeley, CA 94703
(415) 843-7178
8-in. double-pointed needles in sets of 5, sizes 0-00000; lacemaking threads.

Knitting in the North Atlantic

Sheep and wool shape Faeroe Islands culture

by Madelynn Fatelewitz

In August 1983 at the midnight hour, my husband and I donned our winter woolens to take the last ship to sail (until May of the following year) from Scotland to our destination about 15 hours into the North Atlantic (see map below). The next day, having landed in the Faeroe Islands weary and seasick, I vowed not to leave until our departure for home. And indeed, after our final boat ride to the distant island of Suðuroy (our home for the next year), I didn't even venture by car to the next village for five months.

I wrote my parents: "We top the population at 349. We are at the end of a long, winding, uphill, one-way road that leads to sheep pastures and incredible, grassy, fun-looking slides that are actually dangerous cliffs that house birds that people catch and eat but drop (the cliffs) straight into the turquoise-colored sea. It's beautiful here—worth all the nausea!! The sea is a mere 1,000 ft. out our kitchen window. We can always hear the waves crashing on the rocks. And just outside our front door are all the long-haired white, black, brown, and multicolor sheep."

The Faeroes are a group of 18 volcanic islands in the middle of the North Atlantic. As a result of the proximity of the Gulf Stream, the rains are not only frequent and capricious, but the temperature is considerably milder than one would expect for an area that is so close to the Arctic. Because of the fierce winds and rain and shallow soil, trees will not grow. Only 6%

The richly colored lamb fleece at left displays characteristic soft, short underwool and long, coarse guard hairs that the Faeroese spin separately or in combination to produce different types of yarn. The five large skeins show the great range of natural colors for sweater wools. One of Madelynn Fatelewitz's Faeroese neighbors carved the wooden knitting needles for her, and she knit the traditional sweater with the help of another neighbor. (Photo by Michele Russell Slavinsky)

of the 540 sq. mi. of land is cultivated. Sheep graze on the rest. So it seems only fitting that these islands be called Føroyar (Sheep Islands), from the Scandinavian *får* (sheep), and *oy* (islands). Some authorities disagree with this derivation and contend that *Faeroe* comes from a Celtic word akin to the Gaelic *fear an,* meaning Far Islands.

When Norsemen colonized the Faeroes around 800 A.D., they displaced the Irish monks but retained the small wild sheep they found. Through the years, stronger strains have been produced. But it wasn't until 1866 that the last wild sheep were exterminated on the island of Lítla Dímun.

The Faeroes' cultural ties to Norway are still strong, although from 1380, when the Norwegian and Danish crowns were united, Denmark gained more and more control of the provinces. This probably explains similarities in language and knitting and weaving patterns. From the mid-16th to the mid-19th century, the Faeroes were isolated by a Danish trading monopoly, and so the Faeroese culture was preserved. The Faeroes have home rule, and the inhabitants are the descendants of the Norsemen.

The importance of wool

Wool and sheep span the history of the Faeroes. On 28 June 1298 the *Seyðabraev* (*Sheep Letter*) was drafted by a lawman who was sent to the Faeroes to remedy deficiencies in agricultural affairs. The largest portion of this document has remained unchanged. The *Seyðabraev* deals with the slaughtering of unmarked sheep, maintenance of common pastures, penalties and fines for allowing dog damage to another's sheep, penalties for allowing sheep to graze in another's field, and rent for leased land. The penalty for the trespassing of one man's sheep on another's *hagi* (outfield pasture) was 20 ells (about 15 yd.) of *vaðmal* (homespun). Taxes and fines were also paid in *vaðmal,* as were farmers who kept boarders over the winter.

Even before the *Seyðabraev* was enacted, the Faeroe Islands traded. At first wool was exported raw, but by 1361 the islands

were exporting heavy knit stockings. It wasn't until the 1600s, though, that knitting began to be of prime importance. In 1650 the export was 600 pairs of stockings, but by 1765 more than 100,000 pairs were exported along with handknit sweaters. *Seyða ull er Føroya gull* (Sheep wool is Faeroese gold) became a saying.

It is generally believed that the Faeroe Islands gleaned their knowledge of wool, knitting, and weaving from Norway, where knitting was practiced as early as the 9th century. Until 1695, spinning was done with the hand spindle, after which time the great wheel, or walking wheel, was introduced from the Shetlands. The treadle wheel, called the Scot's wheel, was known but never became as popular as the great wheel.

Sheep—Almost everyone owns sheep. Because of the relatively mild weather, the sheep are kept outside all year. From mid-October until mid-May, when the men round them up and put them out to pasture in the *hagi,* sheep are allowed to roam the village roads and yards.

Around April 14th lambing begins. Throughout the summer the hay is allowed to grow, and perhaps two reapings will be managed if the weather holds. Everyone from schoolchild to sea captain helps gather the hay, which, supplemented by grain and corn, will be used to feed the sheep in winter. In mid-June the men round up the sheep (photo below) for shearing or roo'ing (plucking), innoculations, and earmarking the lambs to show which outfield section they belong to and on which stretch of pasture they graze.

Beginning September 29th, Michaelmas, the sheep are separated for breeding stock (these will stay the winter) and for slaughter. About 46,000 sheep (ewes over seven years old and young rams that don't look suitable for breeding) are killed per year; the number of winter stock remains a constant 70,000, a large number, considering that the human population is about 44,000.

Each family kills its own sheep, and both men and women are busy for weeks. The

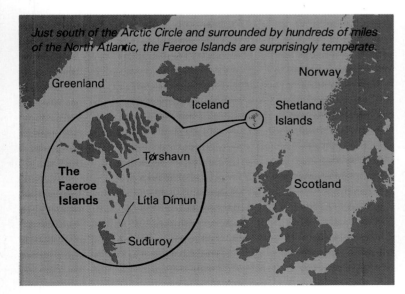

Just south of the Arctic Circle and surrounded by hundreds of miles of the North Atlantic, the Faeroe Islands are surprisingly temperate.

Greenland

Iceland

Norway

Shetland Islands

Tørshavn

The Faeroe Islands

Lítla Dímun

Scotland

Suðuroy

Faeroe sheep are small but colorful, as seen in this annual roundup. (Photo by Dennis Gaffin)

Small and large round motifs alternate in horizontal bands on a sweater in the traditional color scheme (left; photo by Dennis Gaffin.) The alternation of large, curving, light-colored patterns and smaller, straight-edged, dark patterns on a medium ground produces a magnificent sweater (right; photo by Madelynn Fatelewitz).

Faeroese have a saying: "Everything on a sheep can be eaten except the muck, the gall, and the gall bladder." Although not used for human consumption, the gall is given to cattle as a remedy for gall disease. The horns, once made into spoons, are now used for lamps. The skin used to be made into waterproof clothing for the fishermen and moccasin-style shoes for the family, but now it is sold to a factory to be processed for rugs. Tallow is used to flavor fish balls, and to this day, wool soaked in linseed oil caulks the seams of boats.

The rest of the carcass is eaten by the family. The legs are salted and hung to dry in a *hjallur* (wooden drying shed) for three to four months, after which the Faeroese slice off thin pieces of *skerpikjøt* (raw, wind-dried mutton) to put on black bread. The intestines are stuffed with a mixture of blood, flour, raisins, and other ingredients; some meat is ground; other parts are frozen fresh; and the bladder is cleaned and blown up for the children to use as an ornament or a baby rattle.

Around October 14th (Winter's Night) the sheep are set free, and the cycle starts again. But during the long, dark winter and even longer absences of the men on fishing expeditions (fish being the number one export today), the women do not sit idle. They knit socks and beautiful sweaters for the fishermen, others for themselves, and still others for export.

Wool—The sheep produce two types of wool, whose quality depends on the winter weather. A lot of rain and wind produces a high proportion of long, hairy fibers. *Broddur,* the coarse guard hairs averaging 12 in. long that grow through the underwool to protect it from moisture and dirt, make a strong knitting yarn. A milder winter with good grass gives a finer, soft underwool (*rót*) about 3 in. long.

The advantage of roo'ing is that these two lengths of wool may be gathered sepa-

rately, thereby making it unnecessary for the spinner to perform this tedious task. The wool that's taken during *várfjall* (midsummer roundup) is called *várull* and shrinks less than the wool that's taken from slaughtered sheep (*skinnull*). These two wools are also kept separated.

From the *rót* and *broddur* the Faeroese produce three types of yarn. *Nappað tógv* is produced only from the *rót* and is spun on the great wheel. It is used to knit fine clothing. *Samfingið tógv* is a mixture of *rót* and *broddur* and is knit into work sweaters and socks. And *tog garn*, from *broddur*, the strongest of the three, is spun on the hand spindle or, if available, on the Scot's wheel. In olden days it was plied and used to sew waterproof clothing for the fishermen. Today, because it is strong and dyes well, it is used for weaving.

The Faeroese pride themselves on being able to describe precisely a certain sheep in a flock by its color and markings. The sheep are solid white, moor red, light gray, middle gray, dark gray, black, dark moor red, or a combination of white and another color. Names are given to certain combinations. For example, white sheep with black wool around the eyes are *eggsvart* (black egg).

The Faeroese prefer to knit sweaters in the natural colors, several of which are shown in the photos above. Some wool, however, is dyed.

Knitting

Faeroe knitting, like Fair Isle (see the article on pp. 30-37), incorporates stranded patterns and is knit in the round, either with circular needles or with up to eleven 8-in. double-pointed needles. Knitting with up to three colors per row, as in the sweater shown at left, above, adds bulk and warmth because of the stranding along the inside. The Faeroe sweater has no definite front or back, which means that the elbows wear evenly. Unlike Fair Isle sweaters, which employ steeks to bridge openings, Faeroe

sweaters are knit without openings. Armholes are cut later with scissors, a scary proposition for the novice.

Faeroe patterns, which date to olden times, are worked in horizontal bands, sometimes separated by narrower patterns. In 1927 a group of patterns in white and *korki* (a purple lichen dye) was shown at a Copenhagen exhibition. Queen Alexandrina liked them so much that she asked Hans M. Debes to publish them. In 1932, having collected more designs, Debes published *Føroysk Bindingarmynstur,* which now sits in almost every islander's home. The patterns are diverse and charmingly named: Wheels, Kittens, Ring of Dancers, Sheeptracks, Goose Footprints, Fleas, Lice, Sea waves, Hammers, Day and Night, and Hills and Dales. You can use the charts on page 76 to design your own Faeroe sweater.

Stitch gauge has become less fine over the years, and sweaters knit for export use the thickest yarn and biggest stitches so that the work can be completed quickly. In 1900 the gauge was 20 sts to 4 in., but by 1980 it was 13 sts to 4 in.

I remember one night our next-door neighbor, a fisherman, called his wife from Norway to ask her to make three sweaters—one for a man, one for a woman, and one for a baby—for the next day, when he'd be returning home with a Norwegian friend to whom he wanted to give the sweaters. My neighbor lady called over her sister-in-law and mother-in-law, who sat up all night knitting with her. Had the sweaters been knit in the finer wool with a finer gauge, the deadline would never have been met.

Learning to knit Faeroe-style—I was helped with my knitting by many of the village ladies, but by three in particular. Anna-Sofía showed me how to make socks, but she went so quickly that I was baffled. Emma, a Danish girl, who knit the way my Roumanian grandmother taught me—Continental—helped me, and I knit my first three-color sweater with her. Faeroese women keep the main color on the right index finger and the pattern colors on the fingers of the left hand. No matter what knitting method you prefer, to ensure fairly loose strands, hold the pattern wool on the hand that usually doesn't hold the yarn.

My third helper was Anna Steinhús, now in her 80s, who gave me pointers on finishing, measuring, and life in general. Her husband, Johannes, a retired and respected fisherman, using the remnants of the captain's cabin of an old ship, carved three oak and eight mahogany knitting needles (*stokkar*) for me (see photo, page 72).

All of the village women knit, and all of them except Anna, the only one to use wooden needles, have some type of rheumatism or arthritis in their hands, shoulders, or fingers. Perhaps there is a connection between the Faeroes' nearness to the magnetic North Pole and the pains that the women experience. Bamboo needles were

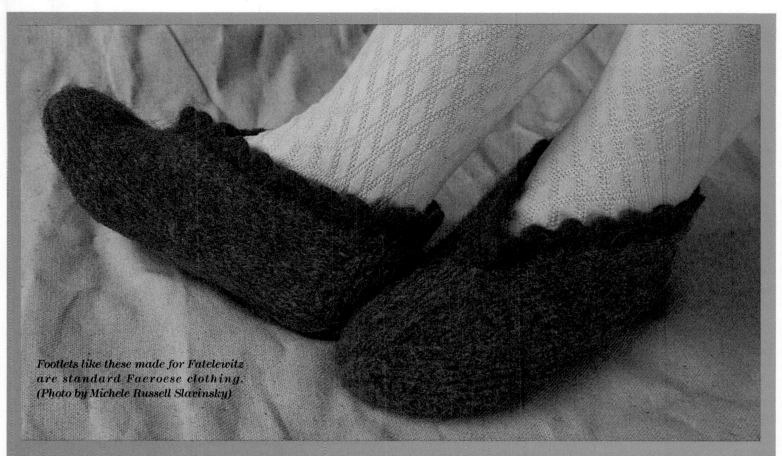

Footlets like these made for Fatelewitz
are standard Faeroese clothing.
(Photo by Michele Russell Slavinsky)

Faeroese footlets

The Faeroese don't wear shoes in the house. Instead, they pad around in knit footlets. These soft "shoes" are comfortable for weavers, add warmth inside boots, and help prevent one from slipping on ice when they're pulled over boots. Footlets also make wonderful bed socks. There are probably as many variations on this basic pattern as there are Faeroese knitters.

To make the footlets, you need 2 to 3 oz. of 3-ply wool and a set of 4 double-pointed needles. With size 0 needles the gauge is 6 sts and 8½ rows to 1 in. Directions are given in parentheses for footlets knit on size 5 needles (gauge of 4½ sts and 7 rows to 1 in.). Increase or decrease needle size to produce desired gauge. To increase overall size, change needle or wool size to give fewer stitches per inch.

Begin at the upper edge of the heel. Cast on 24 (18) sts, and using two of the needles, knit 2 rows. Then work 20 (14) more rows in stocking stitch. The heel should now be 4 in. wide and 2½ in. long.

To turn the heel, work as follows:
Row 1: K17 (13), k2tog, turn.
Row 2: Sl1, p10 (8), p2tog, turn.
Row 3: Sl1, k10 (8), sl1, k1, psso, turn.

Repeat rows 2 and 3 until you have worked all side stitches and 12 (10) sts remain. Break off the wool. With the right side of the work facing you, pick up and knit 19 (16) sts along one side of the heel, k12 (10) sts on the heel, and pick up and knit 19 (16) sts on the other side of the heel. There are now 50 (42) sts on the needle. Continue in stocking stitch until the footlet is 3 to 5 in. long from the center of the heel. End on a purl row.

To begin the toe, cast on 2 sts, for a total of 52 (44) sts. Work in the round on 3 needles with the stitches divided as follows: Put 14 (12) sts on the 1st needle, 13 (11) sts on the 2nd needle, and 25 (21) sts on the 3rd needle. Then slip the last 12 (10) sts onto the 1st needle so the center stitches (half the total) are on it. Knit around until you're about 2½ in. from the end of the toe.

Then work 1 decrease round as follows:
1st needle: K1, k2tog. Knit to the last 3 sts and k2tog, k1.
2nd needle: K1, k2tog, knit to end of needle.
3rd needle: Knit to last 3 sts, k2tog, k1. Alternate plain and decrease rounds until 8 sts remain. Work last round k1, k2tog, k2, k2tog, k1. Use a blunt-pointed needle to thread yarn end through stitches and gather hole together. Weave in all ends.

Some Faeroese women close the toe by alternating decrease and plain rounds until approximately 3 in. of sts are left on the needles. Then they bind off just as they do the shoulders of sweaters. This produces a square toe.

To finish the footlet, work one row of single crochet along the upper edge of the heel and 2 rows along the rest of the upper edge. Wash the footlets and block them so they fit snugly. If they're too big, shrink them slightly by felting.

Faeroese women have been felting footlets, socks, and mittens for centuries. The process, also known as fulling, or waulking, closes all the spaces between the stitches and mats the wool, thereby making it almost impervious to wind and water. It also makes knitwear extremely warm and durable. So, if you want those qualities in your footlets, knit them a size too big and shrink them.

The Faeroese fulled lengths of *vaðmal* by stomping on the fabric in a tub, but you can full footlets in the sink. Turn them inside out, and fill the sink with very hot water to which you have added 1 tbsp. of salt. Dip the socks into the water. Then spread brown soap all over them and rub them against one another or up and down on a washboard. Next, plunge them into cold water. Repeat the hot water, soap, and kneading, and then the cold shock until the footlets are the size you want. Rinse them in clear water to which you have added a small amount of vinegar, and air-dry them. The felting may take up to an hour to complete, and it can be a bit tiring if you have a lot of it to do, but it is well worth the effort, as it makes an immense difference in the warmth and durability of the footlets. —*M.F.*

The shoulder bind-off—Knit together the stitches on two needles as one, and bind off whenever there are 2 sts on the right-hand needle.

Attaching sleeves—After cutting the armhole opening, fold and pin the top of the sleeve over the cut edge, and backstitch through all layers.

Knitting patterns of the Faeroe Islands

Three-color and horizontal patterns

These can be worked with all pattern stitches in the same color for a two-color sweater.

Dagur og nátt (Day and night)

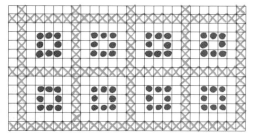

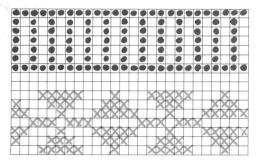

Rokkarnir

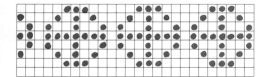

Dansiringurin (Ring of dancers)

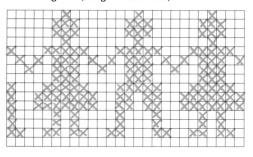

Allover patterns

Renning aftur og fram

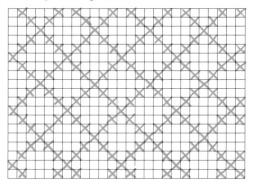

Heila stjørna

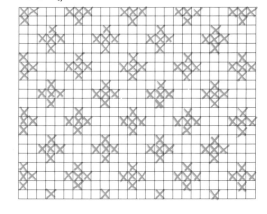

Stabbin

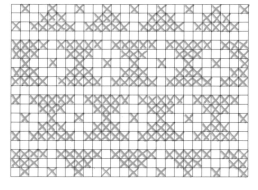

Gásaryggur

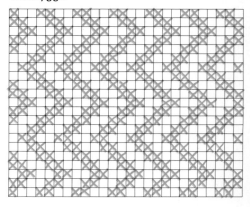

Kettunøsin

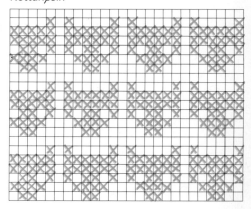

Dimensions for a Faeroe sweater

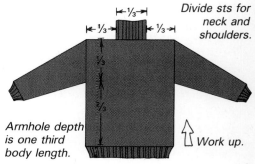

Divide sts for neck and shoulders.

Armhole depth is one third body length.

Work up.

The plan of a Faeroe sweater is very simple.

available, but even though the women believe that the metal caused their aches, they are reluctant to change.

Knitting a Faeroe sweater—Faeroe fisherman's sweater wool, not available in the U.S., is three ply—approximately equivalent to sport-weight yarn. It is not as thick or as loosely spun as Icelandic Lopi yarn. With a few significant differences, a Faeroe sweater is planned and knit like a Fair Isle sweater (see the article on pp. 36-37).

Although Fair Isles sometimes have broken pattern repeats on the sides, Faeroe sweaters are always constructed with complete patterns around the body of the sweater. It is therefore important that after you've calculated the number of stitches required, you make sure all patterns are a multiple that fits evenly into it. If necessary, increase the number to be cast on by a few stitches. You can use patterns with different multiples, but all must fit evenly into the total.

The traditional fisherman's sweater is white with two other colors for the pattern. But color is a matter of choice, and Faeroe women sometimes use a dark wool for the main color and lighter-colored wools for the pattern.

After you've chosen two patterns that fit your total from those shown on the facing page, cast on and knit the ribbing (k1, p1 or k2, p2) on circular needles one size smaller than your gauge swatch, using the main color. Change to the larger needles and work two more knit rows; then begin the pattern. Knit all the way up to the shoulder seams. Divide the stitches in thirds, attach markers (see plan of sweater, facing page), and turn the work inside out to cast off from the wrong side, as shown in the left-hand photo on the facing page.

To join and bind off the first shoulder, work half of the third you calculated from one point and half from the other. Hold the two points together. With a third needle, knit through the front and back stitches as one. Whenever there are 2 sts on the third needle, pass the first stitch over the second to cast it off. Work the other shoulder the same way, and leave the center stitches to be knit into the neckband.

The next group of stitches is the neck opening, half on one point and half on the other. Place them on a holder. Bind off the third group as you did the first. Knit ribbing around the neck on double-pointeds until you have a turtleneck. Then bind off.

Sleeves are traditionally worked from shoulder to cuff, although some people work them in the other direction, and the armhole depth is approximately one-third the length of the sweater. Using the main color, cast the appropriate number of stitches onto four needles. Knit a few plain rows with the fifth needle. Don't start the pattern for a few rows, because you'll fold and sew the top part of the sleeve over the cut edge of the armhole as a facing. So, when you measure the wearer's arm length, be sure to add about an inch.

You can figure the rate of decrease by subtracting the wrist stitches from the armhole stitches and dividing the number of sleeve rounds by half the decrease amount, but Anna Steinhús says the easiest way to make a perfect sleeve is to cut the sleeve shape you want out of a paper bag and follow that. Her method for making the sleeve decreases gives an excellent result. She knits together the third- and second-to-last stitches on the last needle and then knits the last stitch normally. She works the first stitch on the first needle and knits the second and third stitches together.

Now comes the scary part. Press the sleeve top so it lies flat, with the crease at the shoulder and decrease line. According to Anna-Sofía, rather than pressing it with an iron, you should sit on it for a few meals. Hold the sleeve up to the body and use pins to mark where the armhole should be. Cut the armhole opening with a sharp pair of scissors, being careful not to cut too big a hole. Turn the sweater inside out. Place the sleeve in the opening with the underarm seam next to the body and right sides together. Fold back the last few rows of the sleeve top over the cut edges to form a facing. Using a tapestry needle and the main color, sew through all three thicknesses—facing, body, and sleeve—easing in the sleeve, as shown in the right-hand photo on the facing page.

After many washings, the sweater will full naturally, matting the inside strands so they become like a second layer. This will make it even warmer. □

Madelynn Fatelewitz, a musician by profession, a gypsy by experience, lives in upstate New York. She thanks all the women of Suduroy, especially those mentioned here; Nicolena Jensen of Vevnaður, the national museum in Tórshavn; and Danjal Pauli of the spinning factory in Gøtu.

A beautiful multicolor ewe stands on the edge of a scenic precipice overlooking the North Atlantic. Every year sheep, and occasionally humans, fall or are blown to their deaths from such cliffs. (Photo by Dennis Gaffin)

Make a Wooly, Warm Coat

Knit mirror-image Turkish patterns Norwegian-style with Icelandic wool

by Meg Swansen

i like Icelandic wool for several reasons. There's a wide palette of natural shades, ranging from off-white to almost black, and you can knit your way from one to the other by following successively darker shades of gray or brown. Also, because of the extremely long staple inherent to an Icelandic fleece, the wool can be knit unspun. This produces a haze about the finished fabric that blends the colors and small repeat patterns nicely, as plied yarn wouldn't; yet, the fuzz is light enough not to obliterate the patterns, as mohair or angora might. When knitting a 2-ply weight, as I did in my coat at right, you can blend smoothly from one shade to another by working a few rounds, using one strand of the old color with one of the new. And, for areas where you want to reduce thickness, as in the coat's hems or snow cuffs, you can work with 1 ply.

The wool is available in unorthodox "wheels," also called "cakes," "cheeses," or "plates," which have one strand coming from the center and one wrapped around the outside. Thus, you can knit lace and lightweight garments with a single strand (1 ply); or you can work the inside and outside strands together (2 plies) for heavier garments, corresponding to worsted weight. You can even combine three, four, or more strands for bulkier projects. Handle the the wool gently because, being unspun, it may drift apart if yanked. If this occurs, overlap the two ends in one palm; spit (daintily) on the other palm, and splice the ends by rubbing them together. This is also how you join in new wheels; there are never any ends to darn in.

Icelandic wool is also especially warm, since the surface hairs efficiently trap body heat. This 2-ply coat has already been "road-tested" through a fierce Wisconsin winter; not only was it wonderfully warm, but the guard hairs caused falling snow to sit up above the actual surface, where it remained unmelted and ready to be shaken off.

Turkish patterns—If you've ever met a pair of Turkish socks or seen a book of Turkish pattern graphs, you'll understand how intriguing and beguiling they are. I knit the sweater at right first, selecting the main diagonal pattern from a Dover book, *Designs & Patterns from North African Carpets and Textiles* by Jacques Revault (1973). I found the pattern to fill in below the diagonal in an out-of-print Turkish book. The upper pattern came from *The Complete Book of Traditional Scandinavian Knitting* by Sheila McGregor (St. Martin's Press, 1984). The flowers on the lower body and sleeves are my own chart. I added them to break up the small repeat pattern, both visually and for added interest for the knitter. I kept the sweater in two colors so as not to detract from the patterning, but there's nothing to stop you from adding Kaffe Fassett-type color changes.

Since I planned to shade the colors of the wool in the coat, I looked for a relatively simple repeat pattern. I chose Poppy Pattern from Betsy Harrell's *Anatolian Knitting Designs,* 1981 (available from me), because it has a nice diagonal line and because our kids used to call their father Poppy.

I'd been experimenting with diagonal patterns on several pairs of stockings and liked the effect of reversing the pattern at center front and center back. I wondered what would happen if I reversed the patterns at the quarter-points as well. Wonderful things happened. Where the horizontal rounds of pattern bumped into themselves and reversed direction, entirely new, unpredictable designs formed. I had just one vertical center stitch at each quadrant that I used to mirror-image the pattern. Not only that, but the more I progressed into the pattern, the more wondrous and amazing it became. Poppy, as I'd adapted it with my mirror imaging, is both simple and complex. It turned out that the repeat in my version on any given round is 4 and 4, or 2 and 2. In other words, every round in the whole coat is either 4 sts of one color and then 4 sts of the second color or 2 sts of one color and then 2 sts of the second color.

Norwegian construction method—The basic construction of both the coat and the sweater will be familiar to anyone who has knit a traditional Norwegian drop-shoulder-style sweater: straightforward circular knitting with no body shaping. There are no increases or decreases, except on the sleeves, though I did taper the coat slightly, and Elizabeth Zimmermann's percentage system simplifies things even further.

First establish gauge (I got 4½ sts to the inch on size 6 needles). Work pullover body stitches (gauge x desired circumference—100% of stitches) on circular needles from the lower edge straight up to the shoulders. Don't worry about armholes at this point. Cast on the sleeves (about 20% to 25% of the body stitches) at the cuff and increase regularly, 2 sts every 4th or 5th rnd until you have about 50% of the body stitches, as you knit to the underarm. Bind off. Next, place the sleeves against the body side and measure the armhole depth. Run a basting thread down the sides to that depth for the armholes. Sew 1 or 2 rows of machine stitching along each side of the basting thread; then cut along the basting thread. Sew or weave the shoulders together, leaving about one-third of the stitches for the neck opening. Then sew the sleeves in from the right side, and finish the neck off in any number of ways. Pick up the lower edge and knit a hem in 1-ply wool. For a cardigan or my coat (the pattern follows), you use the same cutting method straight up the front. ⇨

Meg Swansen's hooded Turkish-patterned coat is knit with simple, but sophisticated, patterns. Both coat and sweater are traditional Norwegian drop-shoulder knit-in-the-round designs. Swansen produces the elegant shading by knitting with two strands for each of the two colors.

From *Threads* magazine (October 1989) 25:44-49

Turkish-coat schematic, pattern graphs, and measurements

Mirror-image Poppy Pattern at center back and side seams with center st going all the way up.

At center front, mirror-image pattern on either side of 5 cutting sts.

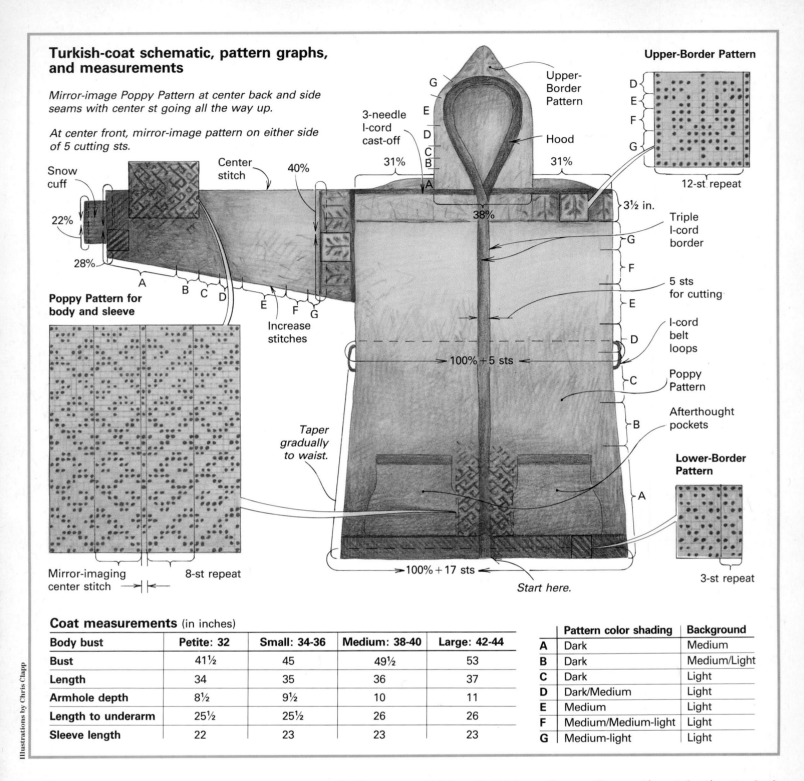

Snow cuff

Center stitch

40%

3-needle I-cord cast-off

31%

31%

Upper-Border Pattern

Hood

Upper-Border Pattern

D E F G

12-st repeat

22%

28%

A B C D E F G

Poppy Pattern for body and sleeve

Increase stitches

38%

3½ in.

Triple I-cord border

G F

5 sts for cutting

E

I-cord belt loops

D

100% + 5 sts

C

Poppy Pattern

B

Afterthought pockets

A

Lower-Border Pattern

Taper gradually to waist.

Mirror-imaging center stitch

8-st repeat

100% + 17 sts

Start here.

3-st repeat

Coat measurements (in inches)

Body bust	Petite: 32	Small: 34-36	Medium: 38-40	Large: 42-44
Bust	41½	45	49½	53
Length	34	35	36	37
Armhole depth	8½	9½	10	11
Length to underarm	25½	25½	26	26
Sleeve length	22	23	23	23

	Pattern color shading	Background
A	Dark	Medium
B	Dark	Medium/Light
C	Dark	Light
D	Dark/Medium	Light
E	Medium	Light
F	Medium/Medium-light	Light
G	Medium-light	Light

Illustrations by Chris Clapp

PLANNING THE COAT

This pattern is suitable for knitters at the intermediate level.

MATERIALS

Yarn: Unspun Icelandic wool, which comes in about 3½-oz. wheels, worked in 2 plies is ideal. It's available from Schoolhouse Press (6899 Cary Bluff, Pittsville, WI 54466; 715-884-2799); or Louise Heite, Importer (Box 53, Camden, DE 19934; 800-777-9665). Sport-weight alpaca, like that sold by Plymouth Yarn Co. (Box 28, Bristol, PA 19007; 215-788-0459) also shades well. Other good substitutes include Rowan New Wool, which produces a stiffer, smoother fabric, and

Shetland 2-ply jumper-weight wool, which feels a bit rough but drapes well.

You'll need about 38½ (42, 46½, 50) oz. of Icelandic wool in these four shades: Dark–4 (5, 5, 6) wheels; light–4 (5, 5, 6); medium–4 (4, 4, 5); medium-light–2 (2, 2, 2). Yardage equivalents are approximately: Dark–1,100 (1,350, 1,500, 1,700) yd.; light–1,120 (1,290, 1,340, 1,410); medium–1,000 (1,100, 1,200, 1,300); medium-light–500 (520, 540, 560). Be sure to buy a sufficient quantity of the same color or dye lot.

Needles: One each 11½-in., 16-in., and 24- or 29-in. circular needles, size 6, *or size needed to obtain gauge.* One 11½-in. circular needle, size 4 (or 2 sizes smaller). One set each double-pointeds, sizes 6 and 4.

Gauge: To save time, take time to check gauge. For a two-color pattern, 18 sts and 17 rnds = 4 in. on size 6 needles in 2 plies of Icelandic held together. I used size 7 for Rowan and size 8 for alpaca and Shetland.

Fasteners: 7 wooden toggle buttons.

MEASUREMENTS

Directions are given for four sizes: petite (small, medium, large). Choose a size from the chart above with a bust measurement at least 7 in. larger than yours. Armhole depth should be at least 1 in. greater than the normal. Sleeve length and coat length can be varied to suit the wearer, but if you knit a longer coat, buy additional yarn.

STEP-BY-STEP INSTRUCTIONS

BODY

Cast-on includes body stitches, 5 sts for front cutting (keep in dark color throughout, twisting carried color in center stitch every few rounds to serve as cutting guide; these stitches are *not* part of circumference calculation) and 12 sts to be decreased gradually before waist. These will prevent hem from nipping in.

With size 6 needle 24 or 29 in. long and 2 plies of dark, cast on: 204 (220, 240, 256) sts, using long-tail (Mary Thomas's double) cast-on. This method is very good for adding a hem, as one side looks like embroidery outline stitch, and the other looks like normal purl bumps. If you consider the outline-stitch side as the right side, you get a natural hem turn when you knit up the hem stitches from behind the outline stitch.

Next round: Join, place beg marker, k5 (center-front cutting stitches), place marker, k 50 (54, 59, 63) sts and mark last stitch for right-side seam, k 50 (54, 59, 63) sts and mark last stitch for center back, k 50 (54, 59, 63) sts and mark last stitch for left-side seam, k remaining 49 (53, 58, 62) sts. *Note:* Work marked seam stitches in whichever color produces a pleasing effect; use chart for center-back stitch in Poppy.

Establish Lower-Border Pattern: Next round: Slip beg marker, k5, slip marker (from here, round is divided into quadrants). Join 2 plies of medium color and work in stranded knitting. Begin 1st quadrant with 1st st on rnd 1 of chart, reading 3-st rep from right to left to marked stitch; knit marked stitch. Begin 2nd quadrant with same stitch you ended 1st quadrant. Read chart in other direction to center-back marked stitch; knit marked stitch. Work 3rd quadrant like 1st; knit marked stitch. Work 4th quadrant like 2nd. Finish chart.

Establish Poppy Pattern: Next round: Slip beg marker, k5, slip marker (from here, round is divided into quadrants). Begin 1st quadrant with stitch to *left* of center mirror stitch on rnd 1 of chart, reading 8-st rep from right to left to marked stitch; knit marked stitch. Begin 2nd quadrant with last stitch of 1st quadrant, reading chart in other direction. Work center-back marked stitch as for mirror stitch on chart. Begin 3rd quadrant, reading 8-st rep from right of mirror stitch to right; knit marked stitch. Begin 4th quadrant with last stitch of 3rd quadrant, reading chart in other direction. Continue in pattern until piece measures 8 (8½, 9, 9½) in. Change pattern and background colors as indicated on schematic.

Side-shaping decrease round: Keeping in pattern, work to 1 st before right-side marked stitch, *sl2tog k-wise, k1, p2sso* (top-left drawing, p. 48). Work to 1 st before left-side marked stitch and repeat from * to *; work to end. Repeat decrease round every 2 in., twice more—192 (208, 228, 244) sts. Work in Poppy until coat measures 30½ (31½, 32½, 33½) in. Eliminate quadrants.

Establish Upper-Border Pattern: Next round: Slip beg marker, k5, slip marker. Work rnd 1 of pattern, beginning with 10th (8th, 10th, 8th) st from *right-hand edge* of chart. Work 13 rnds in indicated colors.

Back shaping with short rows: Working in Lower-Border Pattern, reversing at center back, work across back to 5 sts before seam stitch, wrap: slip next stitch, bring yarn forward, replace stitch on LHN. Turn work (see *Threads*, No. 17, p. 38, for more on this). Purl back to within 5 sts of other seam. Wrap, turn, and knit to within 10 sts of seam. Wrap, turn, and purl to within 10 sts of seam. Knit around in dark yarn, working wraps together with stitches they strangle, and put all body stitches on yarn holder.

SLEEVES

Snow cuff: Using smaller DPN and 1 ply of dark yarn, cast on 44 (48, 52, 56) sts. Join and work k2, p2 rib for 3 in. *Increase round:* Knit around, inc 15 (16, 17, 19) sts evenly—59 (64, 69, 75) sts. Work in stockinette for 3 in. Transfer stitches to 11½-in. needle.

Outer sleeve: With larger 11½-in. needle and 2 plies of dark yarn, cast on 54 (58, 64, 70) sts. Place marker and join. Shade as shown.

Next round, Lower-Border Pattern: slip marker, k1 pattern, k1 background, k1 pattern, place marker. Beginning with 1st st on chart, read repeat from right to left over next 25 (27, 30, 33) sts; mark and knit next stitch. Begin 2nd section with last stitch of 1st, reading chart in other direction. Do 9 rnds.

Increase round: Slip marker, make 1, k3, make 1 in striped sequence, slip marker. Work rnd 10 of chart—56 (60, 66, 72) sts.

Next round: Slip marker, knit first 5 sts in striped sequence, slip marker. Poppy, 1st section: Begin with stitch to *left* of mirror stitch, rnd 1. Read repeat from right to left to marked stitch; knit marked stitch. Begin 2nd section with last stitch of 1st section, reading chart in other direction. Keeping increase stitches in striped sequence, keep increasing as described every 5th rnd 11 (12, 12, 13) more times—78 (84, 90, 98) sts.

Attach snow cuff when outer sleeve measures 3 in. With snow-cuff needle inside outer-sleeve needle, knit around in pattern, working 1 st from each needle together (photo below). Occasionally you must work 2 sts from cuff together with 1 st from sleeve.

Work even until sleeve is 3 in. shorter than desired. *Next round:* Establish Upper-Border Pattern over all stitches, except original 3 striped sts. Replace markers on each side of 3 striped sts. Begin chart with 12th (9th, 12th, 8th) st from *right edge*.

Sleeve facing: With dark yarn, k 1 rnd, p 1 rnd. Change to 1 ply and knit around loosely for 2 in. Bind off very loosely. This facing covers cut edges of armhole.

Sleeve hem: Work 1-in. hem as described below; fold in and sew stitches one by one from needle. Make other sleeve to match.⇨

No wind will blow up these sleeves. After you've knit the inner snow cuff in a finer gauge, knit the coat cuff to about 3 in. Hold the snow-cuff needle inside the sleeve needle with the stitches aligned, and work the two cuffs around as one to bind the snow cuff into the sleeve fabric on that round. Then complete the sleeve.

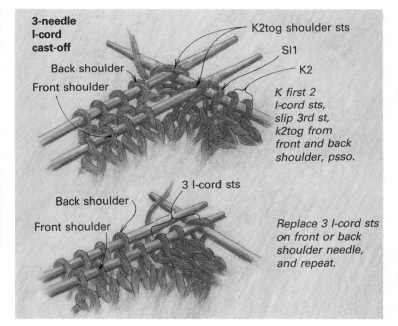

3-needle I-cord cast-off

K2tog shoulder sts

Sl1

K2

Back shoulder

Front shoulder

K first 2 I-cord sts, slip 3rd st, k2tog from front and back shoulder, psso.

3 I-cord sts

Back shoulder

Front shoulder

Replace 3 I-cord sts on front or back shoulder needle, and repeat.

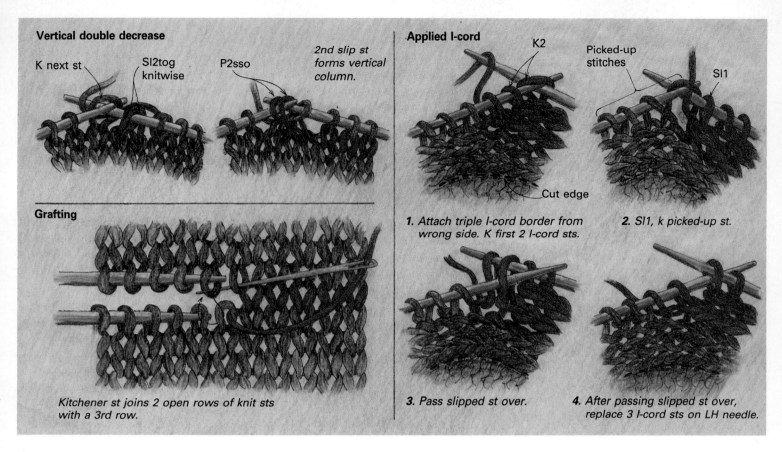

Vertical double decrease

K next st — Sl2tog knitwise — P2sso

2nd slip st forms vertical column.

Grafting

Kitchener st joins 2 open rows of knit sts with a 3rd row.

Applied I-cord

K2 — Picked-up stitches — Sl1 — Cut edge

1. Attach triple I-cord border from wrong side. K first 2 I-cord sts.

2. Sl1, k picked-up st.

3. Pass slipped st over.

4. After passing slipped st over, replace 3 I-cord sts on LH needle.

ARMHOLES

Measure tops of sleeves against sides of body. Baste down centerline. Sew 1 or 2 rows of machine stitching along each side of basted line, and cut along basting thread.

Shoulder seams: Work a 3-needle I-cord cast-off to keep shoulder from stretching. *I-cord,* the polite name for idiot cord, is a tube that is knit with a small number of stitches. Each row is always started with the wool coming from the furthest stitch, pulled across the back.

For the *three-needle I-cord shoulder cast-off:* On 2 larger DPN's, sl 29 (32, 34, 37) sts from front and same number from back. Hold them parallel, right sides out (drawing, p. 47). On 3rd DPN, cast on 3 I-cord sts in dark yarn. Slip them onto one of shoulder DPN's. K2 I-cord stitches, sl 3rd st, k2tog−1 from front needle and 1 from back needle−psso. Replace 3 I-cord sts, and repeat from * across all shoulder stitches.

Repeat for other shoulder.

HOOD

Slip remaining 76 (80, 92, 96) sts to 16-in. needle. Begin round with cutting stitches (kept in dark), place marker, join.

Next round: Slip marker, k5, slip marker; establish Poppy with stitch to *left* of mirror stitch on rnd 1, reading chart from right to left, over next 35 (37, 43, 45) sts, knit next stitch and mark it. Begin 2nd section with last stitch of 1st section, reading chart in other direction.

Increase round: For fullness at back of head, increase each side of marked stitch every 2nd rnd 9 times−94 (98, 110, 114) sts, keeping in pattern and shading, as indicated

on schematic. Work even until hood measures 10½ (10½, 11, 11) in.

Decrease round: Establish Upper-Border Pattern beginning with 1st st on *right edge* of chart, keeping marked stitch at center back and reversing pattern after marked stitch. Shade in reverse of body. *And, at same time,* work double decreases over 3 center-back sts (drawings at top left) on this round and every round 15 times. When Upper-Border is completed, work 2 rnds in medium light, and slip stitches to thread.

HEM

Using 1-ply dark yarn, pick up 1 st for each cast-on stitch behind outline stitch. When you get to 5 front cutting sts, wrap yarn 7 or 8 times around needle (a wrapped steek), instead of picking them up, and continue knitting around. On next round, drop those wraps when you come to them and make a new set. Continue this way for 1½ in. Leave stitches on needle, or put them on a thread. Baste, machine-stitch, and cut center front and hood open. You'll have to do this in stages, as few machines can handle such bulk. Graft top of hood together (bottom-left drawing above). Sew hem in place from stitches on needle and cut through center of steek. Tuck ends in.

FINISHING

Center-front triple I-cord border: For trim and closures, I used Elizabeth Zimmermann's basic *Applied I-Cord,* which she recommends for edging on garter stitch. But when you're applying stocking-stitch I-cord to a stocking-stitch garment, you must alter the pick-up

ratio. You may have to pick up 4 sts for every 5 rnds, 5 sts for every 6 rnds, or even 1 st for every round to apply the I-cord smoothly. I'm sorry to be vague, but many variables are involved: gauge, needle size, materials, which side of the stitch you picked up, whether or not you twisted it, etc. Work a few inches; then scrutinize your work. If the border pulls up, you need more stitches. If it sags, pick up fewer stitches to rounds, or change needle size.

When it's just right, *apply I-cord* around front edge of coat and hood. Working from wrong side, fold cut edge with 2 or 3 vertical rows inside and pick up approximately 20 sts along chosen row at folded edge, using a smaller DPN. Cast 3 I-cord sts onto size 6 needle, in dark yarn, and replace on LHN in front of 1st picked-up st. *K first 2 I-cord sts, sl 3rd st, k 1st picked-up st, psso. Replace 3 I-cord sts on LHN, and repeat from * (see drawings at right, above). Instead of sl, k1, psso, you can k2tog through back loops (this is my current favorite), SSK, or k2tog.

Buttonholes: One application of I-cord isn't enough to prevent a long stocking-stitch edge from curling. Change to medium color, and work a 2nd row of I-cord on top of 1st row. Pick up 1 st for each row of existing I-cord.

Work 7 evenly spaced buttonholes in 2nd I-cord, using Elizabeth Zimmermann's *Looped I-Cord buttonholes.* As you work your way along buttonhole side and come to a buttonhole spot, work 7 to 9 rows (number of rows depends on button size) of I-cord unattached. Begin attaching again.

This loop may stretch with wear, so add a 3rd row of I-cord over 2nd row in medium-

Working a third row of I-cord trim over the second to lock the twisted buttonhole loops into position produces a handsome, durable edge.

After snipping half a stitch of each color in her coat, Swansen knits an I-cord welt onto the stitches she has picked up along the lower edge of the opening. She works the pocket lining as a flat piece down from the upper-edge stitches, widening it as she goes, and sews it inside the coat.

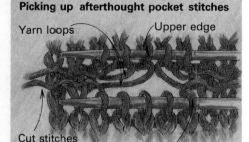

Sewing sleeve into cut armhole

Body

Sleeve

Facing (inside)

Machine stitching

Use mattress st to attach sleeve 1 to 1½ vertical sts from cut edge on armhole. Sew on edge of purl st at sleeve top.

Picking up afterthought pocket stitches

Yarn loops

Upper edge

Cut stitches

Lower edge

Snip one thread per color at center of opening, and pick sts back to pocket edges. Pick up lower sts. Pick up same number of sts on upper edge, taking visible sts and inserting needle in body fabric above floats, where no sts show.

light. As you get to each loop, secure it with a twist, working 3rd I-cord behind and into twist (photo at left, above).

Attaching sleeves: Sew in sleeves from right side (be careful not to catch knit-in facing). I use *mattress stitch,* inserting needle 1 to 1½ vertical rows inside cut edge on body, going up slightly and then inserting needle into sleeve just behind purl ridge (top drawing at left). Tack facing down over cut edge on inside.

Afterthought pockets: This is a Zimmermann "unvention" that I carried into a previously unexplored area—cutting into a color pattern. While snipping into your knit fabric to make a pocket opening may seem a bit dangerous, you'll be surprised at how safe and easy this pocket is to make.

Try on coat to see where you want pockets to be. Use a safety pin to mark center of desired pocket opening. Mark mirror stitch of same round for other pocket. Snip one side of marked stitch, and unravel for approximately 2½ in. in either direction. Since there are two interlocking colors in each round, you must also snip half a stitch of second color and unravel it in both directions. You'll find the results somewhat alarming. Along lower edge will be a neat row of stitches waiting to be picked up, but along top edge you'll see an occasional recognizable stitch and loops of each color. Pick up lower-edge stitches and count them. Then pick up same number of "stitches" from top edge, doing the best you can. Where there are no apparent stitches, pick up from fabric of body (bottom drawing at left). Try it on a swatch first. I worked two rows of I-cord

cast-off across lower stitches in dark and medium yarns.

With dark yarn and small DPN's, work flat pocket lining back and forth in stockinette stitch on top stitches for 4 or 5 rows, keeping 4 edge sts on each side in garter stitch to prevent curling. Increase at beginning of each row until pocket flap is nice and wide. Knit to desired depth. Bind off and sew sides and lower edge down inside coat (photo at right, above). This trick yields a small, neat pocket opening with a nice, roomy interior. Weave in snipped threads.

Final touches: To neaten cut front edges, fold cut flap inside toward body, tuck machine stitching underneath, and sew flap down.

I gave the shoulder seam extra firmness by working a very tight I-cord on the inside from shoulder to shoulder to ensure that there would be no sagging. Purchased or knit shoulder pads are optional.

Belt and belt loops work well in I-cord. But for a wider belt, try Elizabeth Zimmermann's *I-cord belt*: Cast on 7 sts. *K4, bring wool forward, sl last 3 sts p-wise, turn. Repeat from * until you can't stand it anymore. You'll have a belt with a built-in I-cord on each side of a single garter stitch. Increase number of center garter stitches for a wider belt.

Carve your toggle buttons from a length of dowel; then stain them to match your coat (you can also buy toggles from me).☐

Meg Swansen of Pittsville, WI, is a knitwear designer, a video producer, the owner of Schoolhouse Press, and the daughter of Elizabeth Zimmermann. A video on making the coat is available from her for $28.50 ppd.

Designing a Wheel-Pattern Fair Isle Tammy

Crown your tam with stars radiating from double-decrease spokes

by Alice Starmore

Wheel-pattern Fair Isle tammies are little masterpieces of design and color. This is undoubtedly why they have remained popular since making their debut in the 1930s. Feasting the eyes on a display of tammies, each one different, is an enormously enjoyable experience. But it is nothing compared with the fun to be had in designing and knitting your own tammy. Making a tammy is a wonderful exercise in balancing color and pattern, and it is a great deal easier to knit one of these hats than its intricate appearance suggests.

Complicated shaping techniques are not required to form the classic tammy. Despite its appearance, the hat is constructed like an ordinary bowl-shaped ski cap; increases occur right above the rib, not in the patterns. The tammy shape is produced by the dressing process shown in the photos on p. 88.

Although knitters once made tammies by increasing from the center toward the brim, they no longer knit them this way. It's much easier to start with a "brimful" of stitches and work the widest part of the tammy first. By the time you become involved with the decreases, and have fewer stitches, the needles are firmly established by the weight of the knitting under them. Moreover, double decreases—both vertical and mitered—can create attractive highlights within the wheel patterns, as shown in the photo on the facing page. Increases don't have this propensity.

Each step in the design process (drawing, p. 86) is straightfoward. Once you figure out your pattern gauge, you'll find it easy to calculate the stitches needed for ribbing. You increase at the beginning of the border patterns, which are arranged symmetrically on each side of a peerie (small) pattern at the crease. Then you decrease to the required number of stitches for the wheel and apportion the double decreases evenly to complete the wheel. To get off to a safe start, experiment with a color scheme, and use the instructions under "Working section plan" to make the small-to-average-size lady's tammy pictured on p.   ), which is knit in Shetland two-ply jumper-weight wool (8 sts and 8 rows = 1 in.).

Tools and yarn—Tammies are *always* knit in circular fashion. You'll need two sets of four double-pointed needles in two sizes—the smaller ones for the ribbed brim and the larger ones for the main patterned area. Many knitters prefer to use circular nee-

Tammies are knit in the round. Alice Starmore increases right after the ribbing, works the border patterns without increasing, and then uses double decreases to shape the wheel pattern on the crown. Different methods of decreasing and incorporating color in the decreases produce subtle and elegant effects along the axes of the star.

dles (16 in. or 40 cm long) for the ribbed brim and most of the tammy. However, since you shape the tammy by gradually decreasing to as few as 12 sts at the crown, you'll also need a set of four short double-pointed needles.

Yarn should be fine enough to allow for the delicacy of the patterns. The yarn used in all traditional Fair Isle tammies is Shetland two-ply jumper-weight wool (150 yd./oz. or 241 m/50 g), worked in an ideal gauge of 8 sts and 8 rows to 1 in. If you're an average knitter, you should be able to achieve this gauge with size 3 (3¼ mm) needles; if you don't, adjust accordingly. About 50 g of yarn are required for one tammy, which can be roughly divided into the number of colors used, according to their dominance in the color scheme.

Color—Collect as wide a range of colors as possible. This needn't be an expensive process; even scraps can find an important place as highlights in your scheme. It is an absolute rule in all Fair Isle knitting that no more than two colors be worked in one round. However, one or both colors can be changed from round to round, and schemes can vary from 2 to 20 colors throughout. Regardless of the colors you use, make sure the level of contrast between the background and pattern colors remains sufficient for the pattern to show up clearly.

On the tammy border patterns, the colors should follow the symmetry of the patterns; i.e., they should be mirror images of each other on either side of the center row, which is usually worked in different colors for accent. Normally, the peerie pattern is worked in a single color on the main background shade. The chart on p. 86 illustrates a typical use of color on border and peerie arrangements. The outer rows of the wheel pattern are usually worked with the colors on the outer rows of the borders, and as you move toward the crown, you shade into the central border colors. Since there is more space to play with on the wheel, you can add more subtle shading and/or colors, as I did with several of the tams shown here.

Designing the tammy—You start the tammy by drawing a rough plan on which you can note the pertinent measurements, numbers, and patterns. Then you calculate gauge and figure out the number of stitches required for the circumference of the hat, perhaps adjusting this number a bit to fit the patterns you've chosen. After you complete the rib, you increase to this number and work the border and peerie patterns. Finally, you plan and knit the wheel.

Write down the four measurements that you'll need on your plan. The numbers given in A-D below are guides for the measurements for a child's tammy, a lady's small-to-average tammy, and a lady's average-to-large tammy, respectively:

A. Circumference around ears: 22 in., 23 in., 24 in.

B. Brim (rib) length: 1 in., 1¼ in., 1½ in.

C. Border patterns are knit in the length from the top of the rib to the wheel: 3¾ in., 4 in., 4¼ in.

D. Length of wheel: 3¼ in., 3½ in., 3¾ in. Some variation is possible.

Draw a working section plan of one section of the tammy, as shown on p. 86. It need not be to scale, but it should be large enough so you can plot all working instructions clearly as you calculate them.

Determine exact gauge by working a patterned swatch with the yarn and needles intended for the project. Knit the swatch on the right side only, breaking off yarns at the end of each row. You must do this because the tammy is worked in the round on knit stitches only, and purl rows produce a slightly different gauge. You can use the swatch to experiment with color schemes and border patterns. Don't work the gauge swatch over the wheel pattern, as it incorporates decreases.

Calculate the stitches required for the circumference, which you'll work from the top of the rib to the wheel pattern. Multiply the circumference measurement A by the stitch gauge per inch. If the gauge is 8 sts/in. and the circumference is 23 in., the total stitches required = 23 x 8, or 184 sts.

Fit the patterns into the circumference stitches. The patterns commonly used from the end of the rib to the wheel pattern are an arrangement of a 9-to-13-row border pattern, a 1-to-5-row peerie pattern, then the same 9-to-13-row border pattern, as shown in the chart on p. 86. The charts on p. 87 give some examples of patterns that you can use.

It is essential that the patterns you choose repeat an exact number of times into the circumference stitches so there will be no break in their continuity around the tammy. To calculate the number of times a pattern repeats into the circumference stitches, divide the circumference stitches by the pattern repeat (see chart, p. 86). For example, if your circumference is 184 sts, and the pattern repeat is 8 sts, 184 ÷ 8 = 23. In this case, the pattern repeats exactly 23 times into the circumference stitches.

Not all patterns will fit so conveniently, but there is some leeway for adjustment. If you want to use a pattern with a 14-st repeat, as shown in the chart, and your circumference is 184 sts, you'll have 13 repeats with 2 sts left over. If you lose 2 sts, there will be exactly 13 repeats on a total of 182 sts. With a gauge of 8 sts/in., this means a loss of ¼ in. from the circumference measurement. Since 22¾ in. is still within the range of a small-to-average lady's tam, the adjustment will be acceptable.

Remember that both border and peerie patterns must repeat exactly, though they need not have the same pattern repeat. Calculate the repeat for your intended border

Anatomy of a tammy

When you know measurements and gauge, you can figure exact knitting directions.

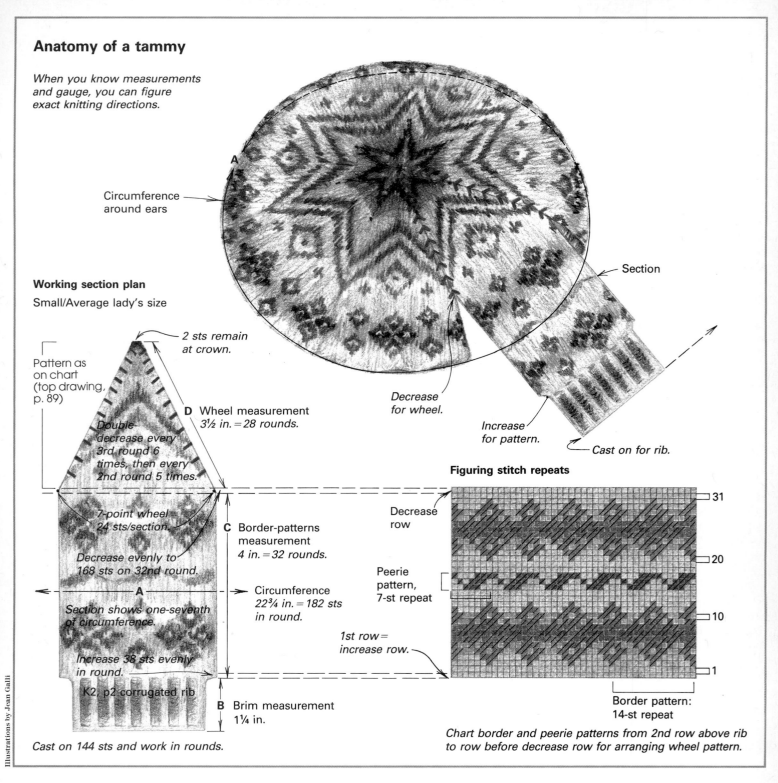

Circumference around ears

Section

Working section plan

Small/Average lady's size

2 sts remain at crown.

Pattern as on chart (top drawing, p. 89)

Decrease for wheel.

Increase for pattern.

Cast on for rib.

D Wheel measurement 3½ in. = 28 rounds.

Double-decrease every 3rd round 6 times, then every 2nd round 5 times.

Figuring stitch repeats

Decrease row

7-point wheel = 24 sts/section.

C Border-patterns measurement 4 in. = 32 rounds.

Decrease evenly to 168 sts on 32nd round.

Peerie pattern, 7-st repeat

← **A** →

Circumference 22¾ in. = 182 sts in round.

Section shows one-seventh of circumference.

1st row = increase row.

Increase 38 sts evenly in round.

K2, p2 corrugated rib

B Brim measurement 1¼ in.

Border pattern: 14-st repeat

Cast on 144 sts and work in rounds.

Chart border and peerie patterns from 2nd row above rib to row before decrease row for arranging wheel pattern.

Illustrations by Jean Galli

---

pattern, as it is dominant. Then work out a peerie pattern that fits. With a total of 182 sts, you can use peerie patterns that repeat over 2, 7, 13, or 14 sts.

Cast on the ribbing stitches. The number of stitches is about 20% fewer (1 in 5) than the number of circumference stitches. You calculate it as follows: Divide the circumference stitches by 5, and subtract the result from the total circumference stitches. For example: $182 \div 5 = 36$, with a remainder of 2. Reduce or increase to the nearest whole, even number—in this case, 36—and subtract: $182-36 = 146$.

If necessary, adjust the cast-on number so the rib will be continuous around the stitches. An even number is correct for a k1, p1 rib. A k2, p2 rib requires a multiple of 4, so I'd reduce the number from 146 to 144 because my ribbing tends to be loose. If you rib tightly, increase the number.

Corrugated ribbing is traditionally used on Fair Isle garments and is very effective on tammies. You work this rib by using two colors in the round: one color for the knit stitches and a contrasting color for the purl stitches. Be sure to move the yarn to the back of the knitting after working the purl stitches so all strands are carried across the wrong side. Also, don't pull these strands tightly across the back, because that further reduces the stretchiness of the rib.

You need not calculate the number of rounds required for the rib length. Cast on and work the rib on the smaller-size needles to the required length. Then, using the main background color and the smaller needles, knit all the stitches, increasing as evenly as possible in one round to the total circumference stitches. If the rib has exactly 20% fewer stitches than the circumference, increasing 1 st after every 4 sts will add the desired number.

Calculate the number of rounds required from the top of the rib to the wheel in order to place the chosen border and peerie arrangements centrally. Multiply measurement *C* by the row gauge per inch.

For example, 8 rows/in. x 4 in. = 32 rounds. Subtract one round from the total because you'll work 1 decrease round after the border patterns and before beginning the wheel pattern. In this example, 31 rounds are to be patterned for measurement C. The chart on the facing page shows an 11-row-border and a 7-row peerie arrangement, placed centrally in 31 rounds.

Determine how many spokes you want when planning and charting wheel patterns to shape them. A 7-point wheel is shown on the facing page. To the left of the wheel is a detail of one section of it from point to point.

Before beginning the wheel, decrease the circumference stitches in one round by about 1 st in 12 to 14 sts (7% or 8%). The remaining stitches must be exactly divisible by the number of points in the wheel so the wheel pattern will fit precisely. For example, if the circumference has 182 sts, and you're planning to make a 7-point wheel, reduce by 1 st in 13 sts (14 sts) to 168 sts. Divide the reduced circumference by the number of points to find out how many stitches each section of the wheel will have: 168 ÷ 7 = 24. If the answer isn't a whole number, adjust the decrease round so that the wheel will fit exactly. In fact, 168 is a very convenient number, since 6-, 7-, and 8-point wheels will fit exactly.

Calculating the wheel shaping—To shape the wheel toward the crown, work double decreases (shown in the drawings on p. 88) in straight lines from the points to the crown, as illustrated by ∧ in the drawing on the facing page. When only 2 sts from each section remain, thread the remaining stitches through with yarn several times and fasten them off to close the circle.

Place the decreases as evenly as possible from points to crown. In order to do this, first calculate the total number of rounds in the wheel: multiply measurement D by the row gauge per inch. For example, 3½ in. x 8 rows/in. = 28 rounds. Then figure the number of decrease rounds and place them evenly, as follows:

• Rounds in wheel: 28.
• Stitches at beginning of wheel: 168.
• Points in wheel: 7.
• Stitches left at crown: 2 x 7 points = 14.
• Stitches to be decreased equal stitches at beginning of wheel minus stitches left at crown: 168 − 14 = 154.
• Double-decrease stitches to be decreased in 1 round equal number of points x 2: 7 x 2 = 14.
• Decrease rounds required equal stitches to be decreased divided by number of decrease stitches per round: 154 ÷ 14 = 11.
• Frequency of decrease rounds equals total rounds divided by number of decrease rounds: 28 ÷ 11 = 2 with a remainder of 6.

This formula may look involved, but it's easy to apply. The figure for the frequency of decrease rounds in this example means

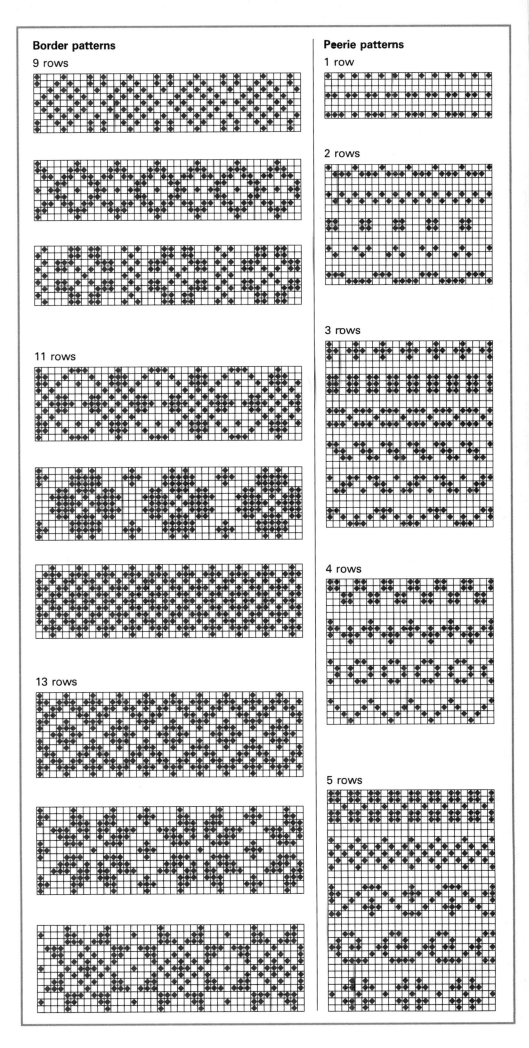

Border patterns

9 rows

11 rows

13 rows

Peerie patterns

1 row

2 rows

3 rows

4 rows

5 rows

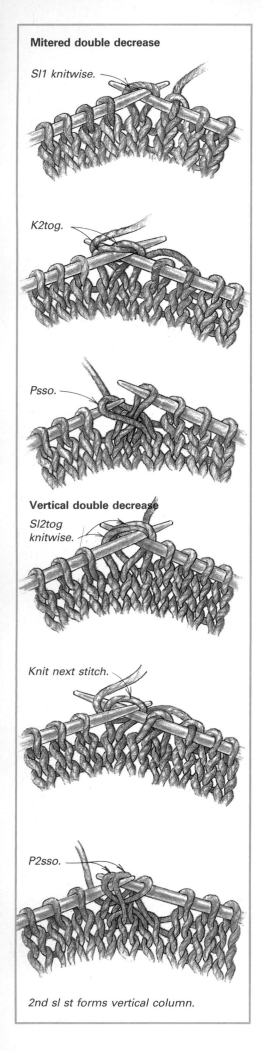

Mitered double decrease

Sl1 knitwise.

K2tog.

Psso.

Vertical double decrease

Sl2tog knitwise.

Knit next stitch.

P2sso.

2nd sl st forms vertical column.

that you'll decrease on every 2nd round with 6 rounds remaining. But working the decrease rounds exactly as stated would result in a badly shaped wheel. Hence, if the frequency of decrease rounds isn't a whole number, space the decreases evenly but farther apart at the beginning of the wheel until the extra rounds have been accounted for. Then space the remaining decrease rounds at the calculated frequency. In this case, the wheel should be decreased on every 3rd round 6 times, then on every 2nd round to the crown (5 times).

Charting the wheel patterns—Once you've calculated the frequency of decrease rounds, you can chart a section of the wheel pattern, including the decreases, as shown by the stair-stepped edges of the wheel-pattern charts on the facing page. Now your chart is ready to be filled with a pattern. Patterns can be varied tremendously, and it's always fun to experiment. These charts illustrate some of my own experiments with wheel patterns, and the tammies knit from them are shown at center and lower right on p. 84. Both of these charts can be used to knit the tammy in my sample calculations. The points of the wheel should always be *charted* beginning at the bottom-right square if mitered double decreases are used (see top chart), and at the bottom-left square if vertical double decreases are used (see bottom chart).

Decrease stitches and color effects—Mitered double decreases (Sl1, k2tog, psso) cause the slipped stitch (on the right) to slant over both the center and left stitches. When worked in contrast to the other two, it is very prominent. The color of the slipped stitch (the one to the right of the center stitch) is determined on the round before the decrease. If you want an unbroken, single colored effect, work the slipped stitch in the same color as you'll use to knit the 2 sts together on the decrease round, as shown in the top photo on the facing page.

If you work the stitch to be slipped in the background color, you'll be able to produce dashes of accent color along the ribs of the wheel as long as at least 1 st is worked in the pattern color before you slip the stitch and after you knit the 2 sts together (also in the pattern color), as shown in the second photo on the facing page.

Vertical double decreases (sl2tog knitwise, k1, p2sso) locate the second of the two slipped stitches in the center of the decrease and on top of the other two. The first slipped stitch is on the right and leans toward the left. It covers the knit stitch on the left that leans toward the right and is positioned slightly below and behind both slipped stitches.

When you work the center stitch of the decrease (2nd of 2 slipped sts) in the background color on the round *before* the decrease, it produces a dash of accent color (third photo, facing page). If you work all 3 sts that will be involved in the decrease in the background color on the round before the decrease and then work the knit stitch in the background color, you'll produce solid vertical lines of accent color along the ribs of the wheel. These lines will have a slightly feathered effect because they'll be wider at the decrease with the angled stitches barely showing behind the center stitch (see bottom photo, facing page).

Dressing the tammy—When you complete the tammy, wet it thoroughly and roll it in a towel to remove as much moisture as possible. Then stretch the damp tammy over a circular board (a suitably sized plate will do the job nicely, as shown in the photos below), and let it dry away from direct heat. This dressing process gives the tammy its final shaping. □

Alice Starmore, who lives in the Outer Hebrides, is a frequent contributor to Threads. *Her most recent book,* Alice Starmore's Book of Fair Isle Knitting, *is available from The Taunton Press.*

Starmore gives her finished tammy its characteristic shape by wetting it and stretching it over a medium-sized dinner plate (left). When it's completely dry (right), it will retain a sharp crease from the plate edge along the peerie pattern at the center of the brim, so she must be careful to orient it exactly on the plate. (Photos by Graham Starmore)

Wheel-pattern charts

Chart for 7-pointed wheel (168 sts) with mitered double decreases

Read all charts from right to left, starting at center. Always work slipped stitch(es) first and then knit stitch(es) from other side of chart to complete decrease.

Key:
- ○ Pattern stitch
- □ Background stitch
- ⌒ K2tog
- ⌃ K1, then p2sso

Working all mitered double-decrease stitches in one color (rows 1-18) gives solid-color lines.

Slip this stitch on row 3. Then k2tog (right side of chart), and psso.

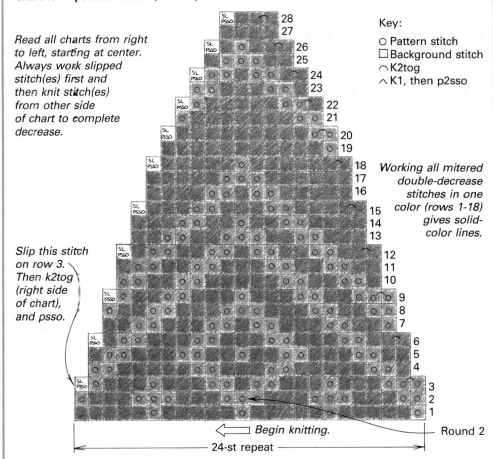

⟵ Begin knitting.

Round 2

── 24-st repeat ──

Chart for 6-pointed wheel (168 sts) with vertical double decreases

On row 3, knit; then sl2tog knitwise (last 3 sts on left of chart). Knit 1st st on right side of chart and p2sso.

If 2nd sl st of vertical double decrease is in different color, accent color dashes will appear.

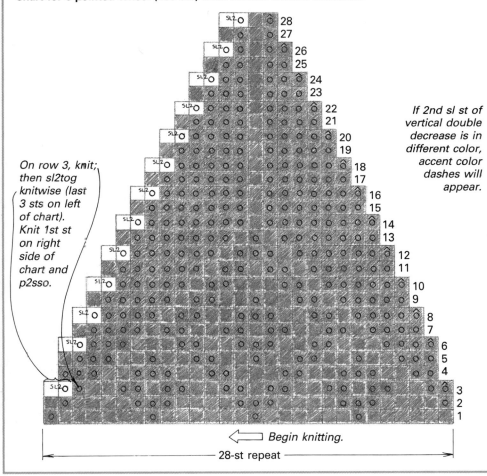

⟵ Begin knitting.

── 28-st repeat ──

Mitered double decreases produce solid lines if all the stitches are in the pattern color (top). If the slipped stitch is in the background color, accent dashes occur (bottom).

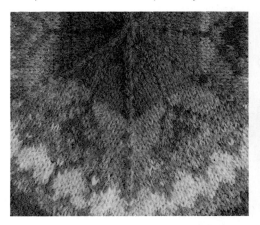

On vertical double decreases, accent color dashes are produced when the second slipped stitch is worked in the background color (top). Solid vertical lines result if all the decrease stitches are worked in the same color (bottom).

Knitting Traditions
More than one right way

by Beth Brown-Reinsel

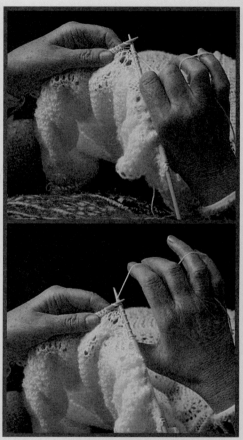

SCOTTISH: *In the Scottish method, Becky Bower-man holds her right needle rigid against her body with her right arm, while the left needle has more play; she holds the working yarn in her right hand. Because the right hand doesn't have to hold the needle, it is free to work more rapidly. Cornish production knitters using this method could knit up to 200 stitches a minute.*

With the yarn in the back of the work to knit, the left needle slips the stitch onto the right needle. The right forefinger flips the working yarn around the right needle from behind, going between the needles toward the front while the right thumb supports the right needle. The left needle then brings the old stitch up over the tip of the right needle and withdraws from it.

From *Threads* magazine (August 1990) 30:48-51

When I began teaching knitting, I always started beginning students with Continental-style knitting. I assured them that it was faster and easier, much better than the English/American style so common here. But after many semesters of watching my students and reading about different knitting styles, I've concluded that no style is better than another, although some have advantages that others do not. For instance, the English/American style produces a more even, consistent stitch; the Norwegian method is well suited to ribbing; and German/Continental knitting is fast.

Knitting, itself, is an ethnic tradition that has been evolving for centuries. As knitters learned new techniques by accident or from someone in another town, these ideas would be incorporated into the local repertoire to be shared and further improved. We knitters should realize that we are part of a long chain of knitters, adding our valuable insights and experiences to the collection of knowledge from which future knitters will benefit. The sharing of styles, whether it's needle position, yarn tensioning, or stitch formation, adds to our craft's richness. We are forming traditions as we knit.

Most of the people shown in this article learned to knit as children. Becky Bower-man is from Scotland, and her mother taught her to knit at the age of five, as do most Scottish mothers. Knitting wasn't normally taught in the school system because, as Becky explains, it's "just a part of life, something everyone did at home." During World War II, girls from fifth grade up were given khaki wool and taught to knit gun mittens (mittens without fingers), scarves, and balaclava helmets for the soldiers.

Françoise Hirschberg was seven when her grandmother taught her to knit. Growing up in France during World War II, she remembers that everything was in short supply, including yarn. Her mother would unravel old knitted garments, wash and

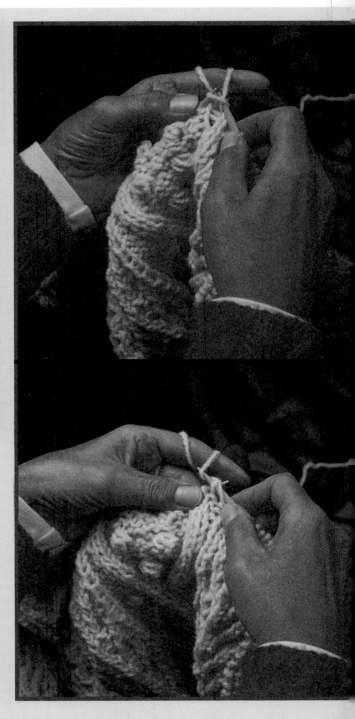

FRENCH: *Françoise Hirschberg holds her right needle gracefully, like a pen, supporting it between thumb and first finger. She holds the left needle either as a pen or in the palm of her hand, depending on the weight of her knitting. Both hands are active, with the working yarn held in the right. For knitting, the yarn is behind the work. After inserting the right needle, the right hand slides forward to throw the yarn counter-clockwise. The hand then moves back, holding the working yarn taut, and with the right needle pulls the new stitch through the old one.*

GERMAN/CONTINENTAL: *Regina Stancill holds her working yarn in her left hand, making this a fast knitting method since the yarn doesn't travel far to form each stitch. Holding the yarn in back to knit, she inserts the right needle in the stitch and moves over and behind the working yarn, pulling it through the stitch and off the needle in one smooth motion.*

To purl, the right needle is rotated over and behind the yarn, which is held in front. Sometimes Regina uses her right thumb or a finger to steady the yarn and keep it from sliding off the tip of the needle as the new stitch is pulled smoothly through the old one.

reblock the yarn, and knit sweaters for Françoise and her brother. During that time, all clothing seemed to be knitted.

Regina Stancill learned to knit in the second grade, as did all little German girls. Her first project was a pair of mittens. One method the Germans use to entice their children into learning to knit is to wrap little presents and wind them into balls of yarn. As the child knits, the presents are exposed one at a time. Regina still knits her family's socks without a pattern, using the "German heel," and her own handspun yarn.

Although my mother didn't knit, I was intrigued by the craft and, at the age of seven, found an Iranian woman who taught me the English/American style. Two years later, a distant relative from Switzerland was visiting and knit my mother a sweater in three days. She used the German/Continental method but purled in the Norwegian way, which she taught me.

While traveling in Israel, Carrie Grayson learned a version of the Eastern method of knitting (which is described in *Mary Thomas's Knitting Book* as the "combined method") from an Arab woman, despite a complete language barrier and no previous knitting knowledge.

The pictures on pages 90-92 show the hand positions and stitch formation methods that these "ethnic" knitters use. All the knitting methods shown are for right-handed orientation and produce the same uncrossed fabric. I haven't shown the English/American method because it is so common in this country. I am certain that there are many more variations to be found throughout the world. Take some time to identify your style, to appreciate who taught you, and to pass your knitting traditions on to somebody else. □

Beth Brown-Reinsel of Delta, PA, spins, weaves baskets, and dyes, in addition to knitting. She is currently developing a correspondence course on Ganseys for The Knitting Guild of America.

SWISS/NORWEGIAN: *Beth Brown-Reinsel holds the yarn in her left hand, but always at the back, making this a very efficient ribbing method. The knit stitch is the same as German. To purl, the right needle reaches behind the working yarn, bringing it forward as the needle is inserted into the stitch. The right needle then reaches over and behind the yarn, bringing it to the front of the work, then through the stitch to the back and off the needle.*

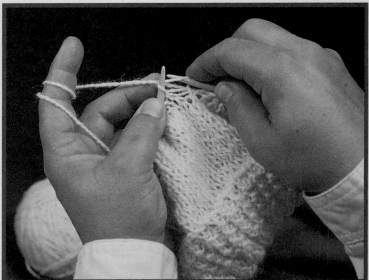

EASTERN COMBINED UNCROSSED: *When knitting this way, the left legs of the stitches on the left needle are in front of the needle, but on the right needle they are in back. When purling, the stitches are positioned exactly opposite. Thus the knit stitch untwists while the purl stitch twists. To knit, Carrie Grayson inserts the right needle in the back of the stitch and "picks" the yarn by bringing the needle over and behind it and then through the old stitch to form the new one. To purl, she inserts the right needle in the front of the stitch, but the yarn is wrapped under then over the needle. The working yarn is held in the left hand.*

GREEK KNITTING: *The yarn is tensioned behind the neck and looped onto the right needle with the left thumb, which holds it in front of the work. Since the yarn is in front, purling is much easier than knitting. To knit, the right needle must be pushed upward through the stitch in front of the left needle.*

To cast on, Patricia Edraos loops the tail of her yarn around her left index finger. She loops the new stitch into position with her left thumb, and then lifts the index-finger loop over it.

Knitting Greek-style

by Patricia Tongue Edraos

In 1967, my husband and I visited his parents' birthplace, the village of Baros on the island of Lemnos in Greece. At that time, Baros had no electricity or running water, and neither the stone houses nor the lifestyle of the people was much different from a hundred or so years earlier. I soon found that my American qualifications stood for nothing here. From what I could understand, the family's opinion of me was that I was a nice girl, but it was a shame that I was so slow.

Our first day in Baros was typical of late April: the old men dozing and fingering worry beads on benches along the wall around the square, and the younger men arguing at tables outside the *kafeneions*. The women stood in groups chatting and knitting. They had no need for worry beads; their worries were fingered into fabric they fashioned on long, steel, double-pointed needles made from wire hangers with notches filed into the ends, as shown in the inset photo above.

I had been taught to knit with the English method, the right hand laboriously throwing each stitch. These women hardly moved their hands; their fingers and the yarn flowed in a single movement. Each woman's ball of yarn was held in an apron pocket with the working end coming around her neck or through a safety pin hooked onto her dress an inch or two below her shoulder. It was then wrapped around her left fingers for even greater tension, and hooked down by the thumb directly into each successive stitch, as shown in the photo above. Between the roughness of the homespun yarn and the high tension, the resulting fabric was like iron. No one used patterns, and it was easy to see why: They could simply knit to size, and, at that tension with the hard wool, the final product would not change. The women examined their work as it progressed, and made necessary shaping or design changes.

During the two weeks we stayed in the village, I watched the knitters and even tried to get a lesson. However, the gales of laughter provoked by my showing them how I knit put a quick end to it. It wasn't until several months later that I managed to learn.

In September on our way to Europe on a motorcycle, we were caught in a torrential rain, which led to my husband getting a bad cold. In Corfu, we were referred to the home of the district public health nurse. While my husband slept off a combined herb tea, cupping, and penicillin treatment, we discussed the upcoming trip through Europe. She insisted that not only were we foolish to go in any event, but we were particularly foolish to go without neck warmers. And she and her sister began at once to knit some. To be polite, I asked for needles and yarn in order to help. They howled when they saw me knit, and added my incompetence to the list of things they already felt sorry for me about. But by now I was resolute. Besides, these women were strangers and, laugh as they might, I would not be exposing myself to familial disgrace.

Under their tutelage I turned out two collars that day. We wore these daily for the next five months, and today, yellowed and mellowed, they are still an essential part of our family ski gear.

If all goes well we shall go back to Greece this summer for the first time in many years. A lot of things have changed in Baros, but if you happen to be there this summer and see me sitting in the sun knitting, you will never guess that I am not right at home. □

Patricia Tongue Edraos is an attorney living in Boston, MA. Much of her current knitting is by machine, but she still enjoys hand knitting.

Index

If you enjoyed this book, you'll love our magazine.

A year's subscription to *Threads* brings you the kind of hands-on information you found in this book, and much more. In issue after issue—six times a year—you'll discover articles on sewing, quilting, knitting and other needlecrafts. Garmentmakers and needle artists share their best techniques and trade secrets with you. With detailed illustrations and full-color photographs that bring each project to life, *Threads* will inspire you to create your best work ever!

To subscribe, just fill out one of the attached subscription cards or call us toll free at 1-800-888-8286.

The Taunton Press Guarantee

If you are not completely satisfied you may cancel at any time and we'll immediately refund your payment in full.

Taunton
MAGAZINES
for fellow enthusiasts

The Taunton Press 63 S. Main Street, P.O. Box 5506, Newtown, CT 06470-5506

Threads

Use this card to subscribe to *Threads* or to request information about other Taunton Press magazines, books and videos.

☐ 1 year (6 issues) for just $28—over 15% off the newsstand price. Outside the U.S. $34/year (U.S. funds, please. Canadian residents: GST included)

☐ 2 years (12 issues) for just $48—27% off the newsstand price. Outside the U.S. $56/year (U.S. funds, please. Canadian residents: GST included)

Name _____

Address _____

City _____

State _____ Zip _____

☐ My payment is enclosed.   ☐ Please bill me.
☐ Please send me information about other Taunton Press magazines, books and videos. (BBBS)

I'm interested in: (check as many as you like)
1 ☐ sewing   5 ☐ knitting
2 ☐ embroidery   6 ☐ quilting
3 ☐ woodworking   7 ☐ home building
4 ☐ gardening   8 ☐ other

BTH7

Threads

Use this card to subscribe to *Threads* or to request information about other Taunton Press magazines, books and videos.

☐ 1 year (6 issues) for just $28—over 15% off the newsstand price. Outside the U.S. $34/year (U.S. funds, please. Canadian residents: GST included)

☐ 2 years (12 issues) for just $48—27% off the newsstand price. Outside the U.S. $56/year (U.S. funds, please. Canadian residents: GST included)

Name _____

Address _____

City _____

State _____ Zip _____

☐ My payment is enclosed.   ☐ Please bill me.
☐ Please send me information about other Taunton Press magazines, books and videos. (BBBS)

I'm interested in: (check as many as you like)
1 ☐ sewing   5 ☐ knitting
2 ☐ embroidery   6 ☐ quilting
3 ☐ woodworking   7 ☐ home building
4 ☐ gardening   8 ☐ other

BTH7